DATA INSIGHTS DELIVERED

7 Proven Steps to Understand Stakeholders, Manage Expectations, and Deliver Actual Value

MO VILLAGRAN

Foreword by Randy Bean, Author of Fail Fast, Learn Faster

Data Insights Delivered © Copyright <<2023>>

Mo Villagran

All rights reserved. No part of this publication may be reproduced, distributed, or transmitted in any form or by any means, including photocopying, recording, or other electronic or mechanical methods, without the prior written permission of the publisher, except in the case of brief quotations embodied in critical reviews and certain other noncommercial uses permitted by copyright law.

Although the author and publisher have made every effort to ensure that the information in this book was correct at press time, the author and publisher do not assume and hereby disclaim any liability to any party for any loss, damage, or disruption caused by errors or omissions, whether such errors or omissions result from negligence, accident, or any other cause.

Neither the author nor the publisher assumes any responsibility or liability whatsoever on behalf of the consumer or reader of this material. Any perceived slight of any individual or organization is purely unintentional.

For more information, email mo@dataconcierge.co

ISBN: 979-8-88759-948-9 - paperback

ISBN: 979-8-88759-949-6 - ebook

ISBN: 979-8-88759-974-8 - hardcover

Here is a free gift just for you!

To get a free copy of a small summary pamphlet of Data Insights Delivered, visit https://dataconcierge.co

Dedication

I'd like to thank my husband and son, who are always there for me when I write. For those who are too numerous to list, I thank you for your friendship and mentoring over the years.

Table of Contents

Foreword 9

Introduction. 15

Part 1: Introducing Data Concierge Agile

Chapter 1: Data Concierge. 25

Chapter 2: What Challenges Can a Data Concierge
Solve?. 29

Part 2: The Five Core Competencies of Data Concierge Agile

Chapter 3: What Does Data Concierge Agile Do? 41

Chapter 4: Core Competency One – Data Accuracy 44

Chapter 5: Core Competency Two – Regular
Communication 61

Chapter 6: Core Competency Three – Equal Ownership .75

Chapter 7: Core Competency Four – Equal Partnership. .77

Chapter 8: Core Competency Five – Trusted Advisor. . . .83

Chapter 9: How Can Data Concierge Agile Make You a
Data Unicorn? 85

Part 3: The Seven Proven Steps to Implementing Data Concierge Agile

Chapter 10: Step One – Listen. 91

Chapter 11: Step Two – Paraphrase 97

Chapter 12: Step Three – Find Problems 113

Chapter 13: Step Four – Provide Solutions. 123

Chapter 14: Step Five – Communicate Regularly. 131

Chapter 15: Step Six – Demo in Real Time for
　　　　　　Feedback. 155

Chapter 16: Step Seven – Deliver Exactly What
　　　　　　Stakeholders Need 161

Chapter 17: Time to Scale Up .165

Chapter 18: What Is Stakeholder-Driven Data
　　　　　　Analytics? 173

Chapter 19: Data Concierge Agile Review 177

Acknowledgments 179

About the Author. 181

Foreword

Delivering data insights is hard work. It should not come as a surprise that companies continue to struggle to deliver business value from their data, analytics, and AI investments. Just look at the data itself. In a 2023 survey published by my firm, only 40.8% of the Fortune 1000 companies surveyed reported that they were competing on data and analytics. And even fewer – just 23.9% – said that they had created a data-driven organization within their firm. Why is delivering data insights so hard?

There is an abundance of data, analytics, and AI technology solutions available to companies today, so what is the issue? The cold hard reality is that delivering on data insights is really all about people. By this I mean that for companies to deliver on the promise and potential of data, analytics, and AI, people must change their behaviors and companies must change their processes. In fact, 79.8% of companies surveyed reported that culture was the greatest impediment to becoming data driven. This cultural challenge manifests itself in terms of people, processes, organization, communications, and change. The consequence is that just 20.6%

of executives report that they have established a data culture within their companies.

So, why does it continue to be so hard to develop and implement data, analytics, and AI capabilities within so many companies? The short answer is that change is never easy. Regardless of the lip service that organizations may pay to the idea and importance of transformation and change, the reality is that people and organizations tend to be resistant to change. When change does occur, it usually unfolds slowly, and over time. Rome was not built in a day. One Chief Data & Analytics Officer put it to me this way, "Our experience is that many people are publicly supportive, but privately resistant, to change and transformation initiatives".

So, what is to be done? In *Data Insights Delivered*, Mo Villagran poses a series of questions to the reader. She notes, "People see data and analytics as a crucial part of digital transformation yet the success rate of such projects is low". She asks, "Why do we fail at such an important part of the whole movement?" Villagran continues, "After a decade of data science, we're still blaming stakeholders for not being data literate enough. Why do we keep failing over and over again despite significant amounts of time and investment?".

Data Insights Delivered outlines a path forward for companies and data leaders, framed as "7 Proven Steps to Understand Stakeholders, Manage Expectations, and Deliver Actual Value". Villagran doesn't mince her words. She is candid and direct, calling out, "the attitude of data people thinking the business can't work with data". She recognizes that in business, the ultimate goal is to satisfy customers and stakeholders. Business leaders are held accountable for achieving these goals. The role of data leaders is to provide business leaders with the information they need to make informed decisions. Business leaders work for the company's customers and stakeholders. Data leaders work for the company's business leaders. As such, data leaders must be held accountable for delivering business value to the company, and if they are unsuccessful, they must take responsibility for doing a better job of building stakeholder trust, acceptance, and understanding.

Throughout this book, Villagran shares prudent counsel. For example, Villagran states, "I hate using jargon. There are too many hyped marketing words for anyone to keep track of. Please talk like a real human being. Confusion destroys trust". She's absolutely right. In a 2022 Forbes article, The State of Data Today, Data Mesh or Data Mush, I write, "The proliferation of technical data jargon continues to frustrate and sometimes antagonize business leaders, as well as sow confusion among data leaders. It shouldn't come as a surprise to any thoughtful data leader that the growing lexicon of data tools and technologies might be off-putting to some business leaders, who want to cut through the clutter and cut to the chase — how will investments in data capabilities enable us to serve our customers better, expand into new markets, introduce new products and services, and use data as a competitive differentiator? Isn't this what it's all about? Isn't that why we are here?"

Villagran goes further and digs deep into the series of steps and recommendations she proscribes to establish equal ownership, equal partnership, and achieve the ultimate objective of becoming a trusted advisor. Villagran wisely observes that it all begins with listening. As I note in the Forbes article, "How many times have I met with data and technology leaders and listened to enthusiastic endorsements of the data architectures and platforms they have implemented, only to meet with business leaders who profess that they just don't trust the data they are seeing – the quality of the data is questionable, the timeliness of the data is inadequate, the relevance of the data to the business questions that are most critical is questionable?" Equal Ownership. Equal Partnership. As Villagran points out throughout this book, these actions provide the foundation for building business trust and delivering business value.

Data Insights Delivered is ultimately a book about taking responsibility. It is a tale of leadership, and how data leaders can and must step up to deliver business value to their organizations. Villagran offers 7 common sense lessons learned based on hard-won experience gained over time by a seasoned data practitioner. She remarks, "Data teams get a bad reputation. However, it doesn't have to be this way. There is a way out, and it's simpler than you expect". This is Villagran's "battle-tested guide", filled with lessons learned, chock full of wisdom, and told through anecdotal stories drawn from her experiences. Villagran's goal is to transform data leaders into trusted business partners. She has outlined the path.

We would now all be wise to listen and to learn from her experiences.

Randy Bean

April 27, 2023

Randy Bean *is the author of Fail Fast, Learn Faster: Lessons in Data-Driven Leadership in an Age of Disruption, Big Data, and AI, and a contributor to Harvard Business Review, Forbes, and MIT Sloan Management Review. He was the Founder and CEO of NewVantage Partners, a strategic advisory firm which he founded in 2001 and which was acquired by Paris-based global consultancy Wavestone. He now serves as Innovation Fellow, Data Strategy at Wavestone. You can follow him on LinkedIn.*

Introduction

I've always been obsessed with resource planning. To me, no matter what I do, it's about how to spend my resources on the things that give me the most return. I didn't have much growing up, so I had to make everything count. Life isn't as hard as before; however, I've grown to enjoy maximizing the resources available to me in whatever I do. I spent the last decade in the field of data analytics, in fields ranging from genetic research to manufacturing. Data analytics is more than just getting insights. At its core, it's about resource planning.

People see data analytics as a crucial part of digital transformation, yet the success rate of such projects is low. Why do we fail at such an important part of the whole movement? After a decade of data science, we're still blaming stakeholders for not being data literate enough. Why do we keep failing over and over again despite significant amounts of time and investment? Most companies have failed to monetize data analytics. And most of these failures aren't caused by a lack of technical talent or resources. They come from the severe lack of stakeholder engagement, the attitude of data people thinking the business can't work with data, and the constant dissatisfaction of stakeholders. All these combined are a recipe for a flop, because stakeholder engagement is never the goal.

Meanwhile, data projects somehow become a status symbol to show how cool a company is. Time and resources are limited. Why do companies spend so much time and resources on things that can't bring them success in increasing revenue? I guess marketing hype gets the best of us. Businesses go after the shiny things, for fear of missing out, and are thus distracted from solving the core issues at hand.

On top of companies having the wrong motivations for doing data analytics, data projects are technically involved, and they require comprehensive business knowledge. It's hard to find people who know both well. Data professionals usually can't lead projects due to a lack of training and communication issues, and the business can't guide the process without a proper understanding of the data. The blind leading the blind is a reality in this field. A perfectly good data analytics project is often destroyed by a sheer lack of communication or the inability to communicate in simple terms. Resources and time are wasted. And data teams get a bad reputation. However, it doesn't have to be this way. There is a way out, and it's simpler than you expect. In this book, I'll share my battle-tested guide to getting insights delivered in seven simple steps.

Introduction

Why I Wrote This Book

I wish I'd been able to read this book as a guide when I first transitioned from academia to the business world. The whole book is based on my from-the-trenches experience of what works every time with different groups, companies, and fields. I want data professionals to enjoy the rewards of their hard work, because I know how hard it is. I want to help you have the career progression and achievements you want. I also want stakeholders to reap the investment and time they put in to get the insights they deserve to move the business forward.

Who Should Read This Book?

If you're a data scientist, data analyst, or anywhere in between, this is the process for you. I'm only a few steps ahead of you, but not as far removed as an executive. I'm in a perfect position to share the relevant experiences you need to hear about right now.

If you're an executive, and you wonder why data projects keep failing and how you can help your team to succeed, this is also the book for you. All it takes is to be committed to providing a world-class stakeholder experience by practicing Data Concierge Agile, my dead simple methodology, which will help you to understand stakeholders, manage expectations, and deliver exactly what's needed.

I Hate Using Jargon

Most failures in data projects are preventable! I want you to be successful and to get all the value you can from these data projects – for your stakeholders and you. There are too many hyped marketing words for anyone to keep track of them all. Not only that, data professionals often push them onto their stakeholders. When they don't get it, they call them data illiterate. Let's be fair. I've been in the field for about ten years now, and I'm just as confused as my stakeholders. It's too much, and the jargon is often meaningless when it comes to marketing rebranding.

In Data Concierge Agile, your stakeholders can be as data illiterate as they want, and it won't affect anything! Stop using jargon. It destroys any true communication. Plus, I never understand it anyway, so I have to resort to using simple terms that a seven-year-old can understand.

As data analytics embraces Agile methodologies, jargon has become even more of an issue. If you must, keep the jargon within your team. When you interact with your stakeholders, please talk like a real human being. Use the word "feature" instead of story. Use the word "efficient" instead of lean. You get the point. I'm so tired of seeing stakeholders' confused faces in the meetings. Don't destroy your communication by using jargon to cause more confusion. Confusion destroys trust.

Introduction

If I Can Do It, You Can Do It Too

You don't have to be an extrovert to be good at stakeholder engagement. I'm an introvert. I read economics books for fun and write sci-fi novels during the night. I never had any official business training. You get the picture. This isn't an extrovert manifesto. This is an introvert's rescue guide.

I've been a statistical geneticist, a healthcare actuary, a Medicare fraud detection data analyst, and a data architect; now I'm a business analytics manager. Communication can make or break a data analytics project. You can have the most well-funded and the best data team. However, without mindfully managing the relationships with the business stakeholders, you'll fail every single time.

I'll share ways that you can engage stakeholders and communicate in simple terms. My passion lies in how we present data to a non-technical audience, which has contributed to the success I've had. I promise that if you practice Data Concierge Agile, you'll be able to deliver successful data projects rather than just leaving them half-baked with dissatisfied stakeholders. Let's dive in.

Data Concierge Agile

To deliver a successful data project, you need the following five elements, which I call the core competencies of Data Concierge Agile.

1. Data accuracy
2. Regular communication

3. Equal ownership
4. Equal partnership
5. Trusted advisor

Unfortunately, data projects are usually missing almost all of these core competencies. The field is hyper-focused on new tools, new models, and the "potential" benefits of data analytics, rather than core issues like automated reporting, user experience, and collaborations.

Data touches everything in a company. A successful data project requires heavy collaboration. You need all five core competencies to be successful in data analytics and offer value for the business. What do you have to do to achieve these five core competencies?

Here are the secrets to successful data projects. I've worked with over 100 stakeholders, so you don't have to learn this implementation through trial and error.

1. Listen
2. Paraphrase
3. Find problems
4. Provide solutions
5. Communicate regularly
6. Demo in real time for feedback
7. Deliver exactly what stakeholders need

These seven steps will help you deliver a successful data project. It's not just about hiring the best data talent, although that's important. And it's not just about getting the best or the newest tools. Finally, it definitely has nothing to do with your stakeholders being data literate.

INTRODUCTION

Focus on stakeholder engagement! You already have what it takes to be successful in this. Believe me, you have more control over data project management than you think, even if you're not a manager or a lead. Everything you do in data analytics is for stakeholders, your customers. I can't emphasize often enough how important it is to understand them. If you do this well, you're already ahead of the curve.

DATA INSIGHTS DELIVERED

Part 1

Introducing Data Concierge Agile

DATA INSIGHTS DELIVERED

Chapter 1

Data Concierge

In data analytics, customer service and stakeholder relationships are overshadowed by new tools and technologies. The field is plagued by bad communication between data teams and stakeholders and constant dissatisfaction. The lack of equal ownership and partnership turns everything into a blame game. It's funny that we're not happy with one another either. I'm often frustrated by different technical teams myself, not to mention the stakeholders. This is a prevalent problem, but no one seems to bother solving it. The adoption of Agile methodologies doesn't fit the data analytics project life cycle in the same way as software development does. The end project from software development is usually a done deal. In data analytics, your end products evolve with the business. In a way, they're "living" products. Agile methodologies of iterative improvement and regular communication still apply here; however, you need more than that.

What Is a Data Concierge and Why Do You Need One?

A Data Concierge is someone who is intimately familiar with technologies and the business, and who serves as a point of contact between data teams and stakeholders.

The most important thing in data analytics is to cater to your stakeholders. Somehow this is a blind spot for many in the field. Why do you spend so much time and resources on data analytics programs? You do this so your stakeholders can have the insights they need to move the business forward. Without stakeholders in mind, you can't do much. The word "concierge" encompasses that concept. What you do in data analytics is highly customized work that requires deep relationships with your stakeholders and trust, at a very personal level. They're your key customers. You work to serve them.

A data project often fails because of poor communication between stakeholders and data teams. To be successful, a data project requires both your stakeholders and skilled data professionals like you to work together. It's painful to watch a data professional, who is brilliant and works so hard, fail when it comes to efficiently presenting data and building trust with stakeholders. Technical people often have limited experience in how to present data and build relationships with stakeholders. And stakeholders have little understanding of technical terms and concepts. However, it doesn't mean you should just accept defeat. I'm here to help you with that.

Every data project needs a Data Concierge. It's not fair to have data engineers manage stakeholder relationships on top of the heavy technical load they already carry. A Data Concierge can ease their burden. This dedicated role also helps stakeholders understand what needs to happen and what data teams need from them in order to deliver.

How is a Data Concierge different from a project manager or product manager? A Data Concierge is technically excellent and can step in to help a data team with development when needed. Meanwhile, they can speak the business lingo or are a subject matter expert. A project or product manager usually only focuses on managing the process, not doing the work.

Where can you find a Data Concierge? It starts with you. This isn't a guide to finding rare talent that no one can find. It's about you stepping up and changing your mindset from being a skilled worker to a skilled partner.

In this book, I'll share my personal experience so you can bridge the communication gap through my step-by-step guide. Anyone can become a Data Concierge and implement Data Concierge Agile. This methodology only has five core competencies, and it only takes seven steps to implement it. That's it. If I can do it, so can you.

Happy stakeholders do exist if you follow and trust this process. I'll help you to deliver your data projects with a world-class stakeholder experience. You'll learn to become part of the value, not part of a cost center.

Chapter 2

What Challenges Can a Data Concierge Solve?

There is undoubtedly a huge communication gap between the business and data teams. This gap seems to get wider each year. As I started in academia, most of my colleagues were technically savvy. We cleaned our data and performed our analyses. I didn't experience any communication gaps because we were all scientists doing similar things. When I worked in the insurance industry, actuaries were skilled at extracting and analyzing data in Excel on their own. There was an occasional need for a data engineer, but most companies had solid data marts for us to use. As actuaries, we did have a hard time getting our data engineers to do what we needed, because they never seemed to understand us. I had to step in from time to time, which was how I picked up SQL and eventually became an expert at it. Slowly, I moved into a position where I became purely technical; I was no longer a stakeholder who possessed domain expertise, in the way an actuary does. I have no expert knowledge of the data I process and analyze. This shift in career focus made me realize that three major issues have eroded the relationships between the business and data teams.

Challenge One: Attitude Issues

You might have destroyed stakeholder relationships without even knowing it. I remember back in academia, a group of fellow scientists was complaining about how hard it was to get funding for their science projects, especially from start-ups and venture capitalists. I asked why they thought that was the case. They said, "The business people don't understand science. They're too dumb to speak our lingo." Does that ring a bell?

Have you ever thought, "Stakeholders don't understand anything we do; we need more training for them to speak the data language?" I'm sure it crossed your mind at one point. However, the quickest way to destroy your relationships with your stakeholders is to blame them for not understanding data analytics. Why do they need to understand the data lingo in the first place?

I know you might feel irritated by now. You may be thinking, "How could you side with stakeholders? You're making the gap worse." Well, I'm siding with them for a good reason, and you might well also be a stakeholder sometimes. Your stakeholders can stay where they are, and it's up to you to guide them in the process. Here is a real story to drive home this concept.

Chapter 2

My team was tasked with finding the right API integration tool for my company. Because we knew little about API integration, we relied on the vendors to demo and help us understand their products. We were stakeholders or customers in this particular situation.

We were in talks with two big-name vendors. Let's call them Vendor A and Vendor B. I don't want to disclose their names because I'm about to criticize one of them. The difference between these two was like night and day.

We were already an existing customer of Vendor A. The problem was that we were trying to get out of this contract because their tools were too difficult to use. For the price that we paid every year, it was simply not worth it. Vendor A wanted to save the relationship by showcasing how good their tool was for API integration. This tool was already included in the bundle we had.

I asked Vendor A why the tool for master data management was so difficult to navigate. To make it work, we needed endless phone calls with their IT help desk and had to install modules in our SAP environment, which was not a small task. It was so complex that we had to hire someone to help us. Instead of listening to understand what I was doing exactly, the account manager was irascible about it: "Our tools require proper training. You don't have the proper knowledge to work the tools," he proclaimed.

"How come Vendor B's tools were so easy to connect to our databases?" I asked. "It only took me ten minutes to learn how to use it while I was testing it."

"Again, you didn't attend the 20-hour training for our tools," he emphasized.

Does this sound familiar? They sure knew how to keep their customers happy. You might be one of them. I know I've been one of them. After this humiliating meeting, we had another meeting with Vendor B, in which we were looking for exactly the same tool requirements.

Vendor B started by asking what our use cases were. As we explained our needs and potential use cases, Vendor B showcased different pre-set connectors for many databases we were already using. They continued to demo ways we could customize these API calls to suit our specific needs. When we asked rudimentary questions, they answered with empathy and shared educational blog posts with us. They thanked us for the opportunity to showcase the tool and promised to demo whatever we wanted to see later. I was impressed with their customer service. Even after we had asked a lot of basic questions, they were still patient with us and wanted to work with us. In short, I felt heard.

This experience reminded me of the way we interact with stakeholders in data analytics. When dashboards or data science projects didn't turn out the way they wanted, were you like: Vendor A or Vendor B? Stakeholders aren't always right, but they aren't always wrong either. As data professionals, you're responsible for guiding them to achieve the desired outcome.

Would you enjoy working with data teams who blame you for not understanding data analytics? Of course not.

Your stakeholders don't have to understand it; that's why they pay you to do it! How can you serve your stakeholders when you don't take the time to understand them? Let's follow the example of Vendor B, who took the time to listen and understand. Customer service should be front and center for data professionals. Listen to your stakeholders and get to know them. Build trust. With trust, you'll be able to deliver data projects with less friction and better collaboration.

With the Data Concierge mindset, you'll be able to see things through the lens of your stakeholders and better serve their needs. There is a reason why we have specialized fields in our society. It's hard to be proficient in multiple fields. Even if you don't really understand their fields, you can still listen and understand what they need. This way, when you strive to be their advocate, you'll enjoy greater engagement and have an easier time gathering technical requirements.

Challenge Two: Fear of Missing Out

Are your data analytics tools really what your stakeholders need? Understandably, you want to maximize your opportunity in upskilling without spending your own dime. New tools are expensive, and you're afraid of missing out. When you read the information on LinkedIn, you wonder how good you are compared to these people. There are many tools out there. To keep up with everyone, you decide to incorporate new tools into your data analytics stack for your sake. Instead of using Power BI, you make a case to use Looker because it's part of the "modern tech stack".

Is data analytics all about the new toys in the field now? Let's not forget it's about solving problems for the business. Data analytics is about positioning the business better. How you get there doesn't matter. If you can get there with Excel, that's fantastic. I know some of you are cringing now. Well, what's wrong with Excel? If you can walk across the street, why do you need to take the rocket? By contrast, if you really need machine learning and have the resources to do so, do it by all means.

What you need to focus on is how to position the business better for monetization. I've noticed that people shy away from the word "profit". When did "profit" become a dirty word? As a Data Concierge, you'll strive to be the point of contact between the business and data teams, helping them to monetize their data.

The better you understand business problems, the more successful you'll be at providing good solutions. Most data science projects have no clear monetization goals. The value they provide is often in limbo. No matter what role you got hired for in data analytics, focus on solving business problems first, not scientific theories. It doesn't matter if you solve their problems in Excel, or something "lame" in data analytics, as long as your solutions are based on sound engineering principles. Be useful to your stakeholders. Being cool does nothing for them. It's all about what your stakeholders need to improve business outcomes.

CHAPTER 2

Challenge Three: Marketing Hype

Sometimes, I think that marketing hype will be the death of useful data analytics. I'm tired of fending off some of the crazy requests I've got in the past ten years. Marketing hype gives stakeholders unrealistic expectations that no one can deliver. Here is a true story of when I was trying to make it as a "data scientist" in 2017.

I failed to secure a data scientist role despite my background in statistical genetics. Imagine this. A real computational scientist couldn't get a job as a data scientist. With three years of consulting experience under my belt, I definitely spoke good enough business lingo back then.

How could I fail at getting a job as a data scientist? Of course, there are many factors that affect whether you get a job, such as cultural fit, etc. However, there is a reason why I know that, on this occasion, it was purely due to the fact that I wouldn't give in to the marketing hype. During my interview with one of the biggest pet food online stores, I kept probing about what kind of business problems they'd like to solve – because they wouldn't tell me.

"Are you concerned with the sales in certain demographics?"

"Are you worried about your Google Ad reach or do you want to increase effort in areas where the sales are strong?"

"Do you need to classify customers so you can sell them more of what they need? For example, so that dog owners will get more ads about dog accessories on their Facebook page from your company."

Silence and blank stares. They couldn't answer any of my questions.

During the following tech interview, I showed that logistic regression would be great for predicting sales in certain customer populations.

"I don't think that's data science," the young data scientist replied, after a long pause. "We want advanced models."

You wonder why data science has failed to solve core business problems and foster monetization. This is just one of many stories in the field. The business, in this case, didn't even know what its problems were. However, they still believed that an "advanced" model would somehow magically improve their business.

I was hit pretty hard by this incident. It's embarrassing to admit that I actually doubted my competency after this interview, thinking maybe I didn't know the science after all. However, I soon realized how stupid this was. The marketing hype has distracted the business from what really matters. You're not the only one who is afraid of missing out. The companies are in the same boat.

It's clear that I wasn't good enough to do data science – according to the marketing hype's standard. Well, that didn't stop me from getting good jobs. I decided to focus on the groundwork in data analytics – building databases and automating reporting dashboards with excellent customer service.

In other words, I specialized in the "unsexy" and "boring" stuff in data analytics.

During my time in consulting, this was the most popular ask from our clients. There was a skill gap for these core needs in the field. It was as if most companies didn't have anyone who knew how to do this. Although this was odd, it was a good business opportunity for me. Looking back, I believe what I chose to focus on in data analytics is truly the core of what most businesses need. It was indeed a blessing in disguise that I leaned into the area where the most value can be offered.

After a decade of data science hype, for most companies, it has yet to be monetized. I wonder how many data analytics teams were ruined by the pursuit of data science. Remember, it also takes a specific kind of business to support machine learning models beyond its core functional roles in data analytics.

What should you focus on now: core functions or data science? This isn't just about making dashboards and pushing data science aside. It's about identifying what stakeholders actually need to solve business problems. Do most business use cases need data science? Probably not. Can some businesses benefit from complex machine learning models? Yes.

Just ask yourself this question: are you doing stakeholder-driven data analytics? Think for your stakeholders, without succumbing to the strong grip of the marketers out there. Who are they to tell you how you should help your stakeholders? There will always be strong demands for basic things like data warehousing, cloud architecture, SQL, etc. This is a solid business to be in. That doesn't mean you should stop learning about new things in the field. I forced myself to learn Tableau, Power BI, AWS, Azure, Python, etc. Continuous learning is a must in data analytics.

When your stakeholders need data science, you better be ready to create models. Before you strive to learn the next new thing in the data field, think about what the shortest path is to provide value to your stakeholders. Start with core skills and expand. Get to know your stakeholders and their fields of expertise. Focus on building relationships with them.

Data analytics isn't for the faint of heart. To be successful, you need to learn constantly and communicate like a businessperson. However, it's also a rewarding field, as you can end up knowing that you have saved people hundreds of hours of meaningless work in Excel, and thus given them back time in their lives. With your help, they can truly be strategic, no longer tactical. With the Data Concierge mindset, you'll naturally do stakeholder-driven data analytics. Moreover, you'll truly understand what needs to be done for your stakeholders.

Part 2

The Five Core Competencies of Data Concierge Agile

Chapter 3

What Does Data Concierge Agile Do?

Data Concierge Agile helps you to deliver a world-class stakeholder experience. It's the methodology you want to adopt for high stakeholder engagement, which is key to your project's success. It's all about your stakeholders in data analytics. It's data for people, not for technologies. Without their engagement, why bother? Data Concierge Agile requires a laser focus on stakeholders. If you want to have a better relationship with your stakeholders, start by improving the quality of your communication with them.

When I first left academia, I knew I had to get rid of my scientific jargon. I was excited to learn how business leaders talk. In the movies, they all seem so eloquent and competent. "I couldn't wait to talk as sleekly as them," I thought. After a few years in the corporate world, I've grown to dislike corporate jargon. I consider it the most meaningless form of communication, worse than guessing someone's mind.

Data projects are complex. The level of skills required to communicate well for a data project is higher than for most projects. You not only need to articulate your thoughts but also to simplify the complexity of the work – without sounding patronizing. Imagine adding corporate jargon into the mix. Even with the most advanced translator, you wouldn't be able to understand what in the world is going on.

If an audience doesn't know what's going on, what are you doing there? People who use corporate jargon probably don't plan to solve any problems; instead, they often use it as a shield for not doing anything. To make matters worse, the data analytics field has slowly adopted various Agile methodologies. Don't get me wrong, Agile is good. However, it's overkill to repackage the core Agile methodology features into a series of certifications and courses. The market keeps creating variations in Agile project management methodologies, like wildfire.

Data Concierge Agile has no jargon, no ceremonial meetings, and no required certifications. It's so simple that there are only five core competencies and seven simple steps required to implement it. The principles are easy to understand at the third-grade level. You won't have any problem when you use it in a multilingual company. It's my goal to make data project management so simple that you can focus on doing what you do best – analyzing data and gaining insights from it. Now let's dive into the core competencies of Data Concierge Agile.

Chapter 4

Core Competency One – Data Accuracy

Do you trust your data to make important business decisions? It's normal to be dubious about this. Having worked in fraud detection, I've grown to be paranoid about any data coming my way. The data presented has to be tripled checked, and sometimes more. You don't need me to tell you that you shouldn't present erroneous data. How can you do that without expert knowledge of the source of your data? It's quite simple – ask your stakeholders to help you. They absolutely need to be involved in this process. Depending on your use cases, your stakeholders will be able to tell you if your data is "accurate" enough to be meaningful.

Your stakeholders are the experts in their fields. Remember, any data analytics project is a partnership. You don't have to do this on your own. Invite them to solve problems with you. They'll appreciate that. From my personal experience, they love it! You might feel the business sometimes just dumps projects on you and leaves. However, it isn't always the case. When you help automate some reports they have been preparing manually for years, they're personally invested in you getting it right. Their career is on the line too. When you invite them to solve data quality issues with you, it gives them a chance to share ownership. It makes sure the final products are of the highest quality. Through these collaborative activities, you can build trust between your stakeholders and you.

So how accurate should your data be? Again, there isn't a universal answer. It depends on your specific use cases. Let's look at the motivations behind some of the common scenarios so you can determine how accurate it should be with your stakeholders.

Insight-Driven vs. Audit-Driven

Are you looking for a general trend in your data or to verify the results of your observations? In other words, Is it insight-driven or audit-driven? If you can't answer this question, don't worry, because it's often both. Although the world is filled with messy data, it's still helpful to decide the level of accuracy you require using these two high-level categories. Just remember that there is no perfect data. Your dataset will never be comprehensive enough to make any universal inference. However, that doesn't mean you can't use it to your advantage. Data with errors isn't always useless if you use it correctly.

There are endless ways we can gain insights from various types of available data. Let's dive into a few high-level categories to serve as examples to guide you.

Insight-Driven Projects

BI Projects Using Commercial Transactional Data

Business use cases are mostly insight-driven and intended to be a tool that helps the user to make sound business decisions. You need to be accurate to an extent, but being off by $500 out of $5 million won't affect anything. For example, you plan to run Google Ads in Los Angeles and summarize the total sales amount by zip code area in a BI dashboard. Let's say zip code areas near Hollywood generated $3,302,002 of sales in total, and the rest of the areas in Los Angeles had a total of $1,200,976. When your stakeholders try to decide which zip code areas they should place more Google ads in to increase revenue, it's clear that areas outside of Hollywood could use some help. If your sales records come into your database in real time, by the time you present them to your stakeholders, the numbers will be different. This is acceptable, since all you want to know is which area sales are low in, making it a potential target for more ads.

The level of the accuracy of your data is totally at the discretion of your stakeholders and your use cases. You must involve them in a project early on to look at your results, so they can do a gut check. Don't underestimate this simple step. Data people aren't usually skilled in a specific field; they're mostly only experts in analytics tools. You need that business context from them every single time. Even if you're experienced in a particular field, please still involve them. It takes a "village" to deliver a data project. Collaboration builds trust. I don't think anyone would say "no" to too much trust.

Data Science Projects

Most data science projects are data-driven as well. The word "science" in data science doesn't carry the same academic weight as in the business world. In statistical genetics research, for example, the results from those research projects can affect patients, drug discoveries, and treatment options. The ramifications can sometimes be a matter of life and death. By contrast, data science in business doesn't require the same level of rigor, although that doesn't mean you should become complacent. It still involves a lot of money and people's livelihoods.

When a data science project uses statistics to infer results, you should explain them to your stakeholders in simple and relative terms. Use an analogy whenever you can. In this way, you can also show them that a model is just a model. With different data, you'll see different results. Teach them how to interpret the data for business decisions. Here is an example of what you could say and what it would be best not to say in a pretend marketing program in New York City for selling jewelry.

Dos:

"If we increase our marketing effort in areas near Central Park, we might double our sales in our luxury jewelry line, according to the model using our current sales data."

Don'ts:

"The P value of this model is 0.00007552. We think we have the right categorical variables. After a few rounds of testing, we found that the sales volume will be about $2.4M if we increase our marketing effort in these zip code areas in New York City."

Please use simple and relative terms. It's also a form of insurance to protect your credibility. Don't try to sound smart. You're already smart. Please explain the results to your stakeholders at the third-grade level.

There is also another important reason to use simple and relative terms when you explain these models to your stakeholders. Models and data are never going to be perfect. If you provide absolute answers, your stakeholders will demand absolute results. It's important to manage that expectation.

Audit-Driven Projects

BI Projects Using Financial or Insurance Claim Data

When you're making a dashboard to show revenue using financial records, you need to match numbers to the penny. Although BI dashboards mostly show high-level totals, rounding and discrepancies in FX rates can have a huge impact on totals if you aren't careful.

Insurance claims are the same. In the insurance industry, actuaries rely on how many claims were filed in the previous years, in order to predict how many claims will be filed this year. When members in an insurance plan spent more last year, it'll increase the premiums in the coming year. If your trend for claim volume was wrong, it could affect the premiums next year. This has both legal and political ramifications. Imagine the poor senior citizens were forced to pay more premiums in Medicare, which is a senior medical benefit funded by tax dollars in the United States. If you remember an episode of *Seinfeld* where Uncle Leo was talking about how the grandma lived on a very fixed income, bear in mind your analysis could impact people like that. When Medicare premiums go up, they can make headlines. The numbers have to be right! Data professionals are usually the last defense against data errors. You should triple-check your numbers at all times!

Law Enforcement and Fraud Detection Projects

Having worked in fraud detection for Medicare, I learned the seriousness of data accuracy on all fronts. For instance, your data will be used to indict people in court. Will an estimated fraud amount be a legitimate piece of evidence to arrest people? No! This field is serious about data quality checks. You'll be assigned at least two of your colleagues to double-check your work – plus there is a final managerial approval stage before anything goes to law enforcement agencies such as the OIG, the FBI, etc. There are rigorous processes in place for every step of the data analysis you do.

If data science models are applied here, the models are usually used to find leads for fraud, not evidence of fraud. It's important to remember that correlation is not causation. I repeat – correlation is not causation. People are biased. You just need to remind your stakeholders and yourself what your goals are for your use cases. Beyond fraud detection, the same principle applies. You should start from a neutral point of view to see what your limited dataset can tell you about the business and the market. If the goal of your use case is to confirm what you've already observed in the industry, the results are purely used for confirmation. It can nonetheless be a powerful tool to boost confidence in your business decisions. If your goal is to find market trends without too much prior knowledge, you need to interpret the data as it is.

You'll run into people who desperately want the data to show them what they want to see. People like this are everywhere. It can be an overzealous law enforcement agent or a head of marketing who wants to implement an aggressive growth strategy. Your job is to help them see the data as it is. Stay neutral. It can be very tempting to go along with what they want. Stay professional. If necessary, reach out to your legal department and have lawyers help you with some of these difficult situations.

I was forced to forge data once when I was in consulting. I called the corporate lawyer on the very same day, and the lawyer helped me resolve the situation quickly and smoothly. There is always help available. Don't suffer alone. It isn't worth risking your reputation to build up someone else's fake reputation.

Both Insight-Driven and Audit-Driven Projects

When a project is a hybrid of both, data accuracy becomes even more important. You need to get it right. You have to get it right. I remember an analyst who I used to work with had a lot of errors in her code, documentation, and summaries presented to the stakeholders. She'd make similar mistakes constantly. I tried to understand why this happened so often. I asked her what she thought the source of these errors was. She said she was just always so confused and tired. She admitted that she wasn't very good with numbers.

I truly believe that she understood how important it is to present correct numbers. However, I also believe she shouldn't be a data analyst, given that her talent clearly lies somewhere else other than dealing with numbers. That might sound harsh. However, my real point is that it's best to do something that caters to your strengths. She didn't enjoy digging into the data for hours at a time. However, she was very personable, and she enjoyed building relationships with others. I know she could have become a successful HR professional. However, she had chosen a career in data analytics, for reasons I couldn't understand.

Although this isn't a careers book, it's important to point out that you should understand your strengths and nurture them. A career in data analytics isn't for everyone. In a similar way, it would have been a terrible idea for me to become a basketball player because I'm too short.

Now let's go back to the importance of providing accurate analysis. During my time in fraud detection, I once had to redo an analysis because I was a few cents off. Imagine you price Medicare Part D plans, which is a drug description program for senior citizens in the United States, and your data science algorithm result is incorrect by half of a percent. That has a huge impact on Medicare Part D plans. Premiums for these plans only differ by a few cents. It shows how competitive your pricing has to be. It might therefore be best to avoid insight-driven data science models for pricing insurance in general.

Here is another example of when a highly regulated dataset is used in an insight-driven project.

Your task is to predict the percentage of genetic testing fraud for the next year in Medicare expenditure using the past three years of data. That is a decent amount of data for a project like that. You can use several statistical models to predict fraud. However, you need to find out what happened in the last three years in Medicare policy ruling on genetic testing claims.

Medicare policies change on an annual, monthly, and sometimes weekly basis depending on what types of benefits you're looking at. For genetic testing specifically, you want to know if it has become harder to get claims paid by Medicare over the past three years. Has law enforcement targeted more labs doing fraudulent genetic testing during this time? Have criminals switched focus to other kinds of fraud such as homecare etc.? Answers to these questions will help you understand if your data is worth anything. Here is why. If law enforcement has been cracking down on these labs doing fraudulent genetic testing, criminals are likely to change the fraud scheme to something else. So your data might predict a high percentage of fraud for the next year based on the last three years of data. However, the criminals have already switched gears and moved on to some other healthcare benefits. Therefore, you won't find a lot of fraud in the coming year even if your data and your model are correct.

The real world won't work according to your predictions. Your model can't predict political changes in the healthcare market. Let's say you got lucky, and there were no changes in law enforcement's focus or criminal behaviors. Your prediction on the percentage of genetic testing fraud was indeed correct. The government realized how much fraud would take place in genetic testing and decided to reduce the payout on genetic tests for the next year. This means that poor senior citizens in the United States might not get genetic tests when they needed them because the government reduced the benefits available for that. Now you can see you're playing Jenga with data. When you safely move one piece to the top, another piece seems to fall apart unexpectedly.

Be careful with the real-world applications of your findings. These are the things people don't talk about enough on LinkedIn or any other social media platforms. Beyond the exciting AI and new tools in the field, we have very few mechanisms to safeguard against such implications stemming from data errors and misuse of statistical models. It almost always falls on experienced data professionals to do something about it. Although it can feel like a huge burden, you can always seek help. That is why I'd like you to embrace Data Concierge Agile. When you become the point of contact between technologies and end users, you can manage these situations better, with more help and more insights as to what you can do.

How Can You Trust Your Data to Make Important Business Decisions?

As data professionals, you need to involve your stakeholders in the process of quality checks. The business context is crucial for trust and the level of accuracy needed. Talk to your stakeholders in relative terms unless you're both working to verify a specific result in an audit-like activity. If you don't know how to judge the quality and the results of the data, ask them for help! I know it seems that I'm repeating myself. It's true. I really want you to remember how important it is to ask them to help you.

I'd always been a stakeholder doing technical things. Last year, I decided to leave the world of healthcare insurance claims and join a pharmaceutical manufacturing company. The data in manufacturing is different from insurance claims, to say the least. For the first time, I felt completely lost in new types of data. On my own, I couldn't make any sound judgment on financial records, which were the data we needed to render in Power BI.

How can you manage to not look like an idiot and still deliver projects? Ask your stakeholders for help. Most of them never expect you to be a domain expert although it's highly recommended. They freely taught me about corporate finance, accounting terms, and so on. I also studied alone in my free time to catch up. I may never have the "data" sense my stakeholders have. However, I gain the benefit of leveraging their expertise to deliver projects and build trust through these mentoring relationships. Stakeholders feel part of the process, and you get to learn a lot about a new field. What is not to like? What do you have to lose by asking for help? By working together, your stakeholders and you will regain your faith in your data and use it to make sounder business decisions.

How Do You Ensure Data Quality?

There is never a perfect answer to this question. Every company has different processes and types of data. The general rule is this – you need at least two people to check your work, one person from your team as a technical checker and another person who is one of your stakeholders. Let's dive into different scenarios to explore ways to ensure data quality.

Regular Data Requests

Here is a simple analysis task as an example. You need to query against a database and get some data back. The urge is to share it immediately with the requester and be done with it. However, take a moment to interpret the data, no matter how simple it is. Make it a habit. I can't tell you how many times vendors have given me data comprised of exactly 1000 rows. Why? Because it's the standard query from the MS SQL database.

The next step is to have your technical colleague check your work. It doesn't have to be an official code review. You can simply ask them to perform the same query and see if they arrive at the same answer. You can send it to the requester after this simple check. The data requester is usually a stakeholder in a junior or senior role, probably not someone from the C-suite. You should feel comfortable presenting the result as a draft and asking this stakeholder to verify the data with their industry or business experience.

When I work with actuaries or accountants, they can tell immediately how far off my answers are because they know the data well. That is something you want to leverage. These are precious experiences and insights you can only get from your stakeholders. You better make sure that, by the time, your data shows up at a CEO's meeting, it's solid and accurate.

You may make a mistake here and there. That is fine because no one is perfect. However, if you regularly miss something, you'll be known for it. Don't be a careless analyst. It's easy to become complacent when you've been doing the same thing for a while. Data never ceases to surprise you.

When I was doing statistical genetic research in graduate school, I performed a logistic regression on gene correlations with Alzheimer's disease. I've done this regression analysis many times before. In statistics, a value of one means a patient from the experiment group has Alzheimer's and a value of zero means a patient from the control group does not.

When the computer program was done processing the data, I was amazed by the high correlations I found with a lot of genes in our samples. It was a scientific miracle! That afternoon, I presented my work with untamed joy during a lab meeting.

My professor became suspicious of my results. She'd been in the field, studying Alzheimer's disease for over 30 years. Within 15 minutes, the graduate student, who had given me the data, told the group that he had "accidentally" labeled a value of one as the control group and a value of zero as the experiment group in the data.

Up to this day, I still can't understand how stupid this whole event was. Who would label the control group as one? I was at Washington University in St. Louis, one of the top research centers for human genetics research. How could this happen? However, it happened. This is why it's crucial to find someone who knows the data, the field, or the business to check your answers. Remember, find at least one technical checker and one business checker for all of your data tasks if you can. This is a must. If I were a Mandalorian, I'd say, "This is the way".

Chapter 4

BI Dashboards

Although BI dashboards are visual tools, it doesn't mean you don't need to check the numbers. The numbers on dashboards are dynamic on Power BI or Tableau. It's quite a challenge to check against a static Excel spreadsheet or query on demand to thoroughly conduct a comprehensive data check.

What you can do is to create a canned query script in whatever language you feel comfortable using. Recreate the answers from each dashboard view in your queries. You can write a dynamic query to do that. Now, there are many tools available for this kind of task. Make good use of these tools. Set this step up as part of your dashboard-building process. I usually ask the stakeholders to try breaking my dashboards so I know how good they are. Click on stuff like crazy to see if I missed anything. You'll go through a few rounds of this. It's necessary. Don't skip it. It's hard work in data analytics. This is also teamwork. Don't do this alone. Invite your stakeholders to help you.

Data Engineering Tasks

Thanks to modern data tools, it's getting easier and more manageable to build a data pipeline with automatic scheduling and orchestration from different data sources. There are a lot of templates out there you can use like ones that eliminate duplicates, nulls, etc. However, none of them is as important as examining the final results in a business context.

Your pipeline can run most efficiently, and your data can still be wrong. I usually opt to build a simple dashboard for myself to see the final results. It's also very helpful to show it to your stakeholders, because it's too hard for them to look at the pipelines with you. The coding usually overwhelms them, unless they're experienced in coding themselves.

As a data engineer, you can lean on the data analyst on your team. They know just the right amount of technical things to help you gain a good sense of the data. It can sometimes feel like you're building a data pipeline for no one. Nonetheless, still get as much business context as possible from the business.

Data Science Models

It's hard to judge the accuracy of data science models. It depends solely on your use case. Sometimes, good enough is good enough. Let's look at an example using online watch sales data. If your model is used to predict sales of a commercial product like watches online, the sales data comes into your database in real time, meaning the total sales change whenever a purchase is made. If that's the case, you just need to know the rough number of sales over whatever time interval your stakeholder cares about.

In this example, you have wiggle room for statistical errors using any models. You're looking for a general trend, an insight-driven model, rather than using it for financial audits. You should still have data checks, such as comparing last year's sales data if it is available, consulting with your stakeholders, and looking at marketing trends. Through this data check exercise, you'll have a better understanding of why you might have an influx of sales and know that it's not caused by data errors you don't know about. For example, it makes sense if you see you have an influx of sales around Christmas time. If you have a huge influx of sales during off-season months, something might be wrong. Test a few scenarios and learn the business from your stakeholders before presenting the final model. My professor from graduate school always said it's 80% data cleaning and 20% fun analysis.

Now let's move on to an example where you use financial records from a private bank to see who is most likely to get loans from you. You're looking for a trend. However, this needs to be accurate. Banking is a highly regulated field. Even if it's a model to unearth potential customers, which has an indirect impact on the banking business, this doesn't mean that you can be complacent with your results. You need to match numbers to the penny. Any data in a highly regulated industry needs to be as accurate as possible. The room for error is next to none, because your results can have a huge impact on a business in this kind of industry.

Again, involve your stakeholders to help you understand what the general trends usually look like. You can apply all the descriptive statistics to "check" the data such as checking nulls, and duplicate rows, and call it good. However, I have to say that this is simply insufficient. It's a lazy way of doing your job. Please just talk to a real person about your data quality. There are usually so many blind spots that you can't anticipate, like the one I experienced when I was doing genetic research. Involve your stakeholder from the get-go.

Chapter 5

Core Competency Two – Regular Communication

Although all five core competencies are equally important. This one is particularly hard to navigate and implement. I'll walk you through every situation I've run into with examples in the third part of the book. Now let's talk about why you need regular communication with your stakeholders. It's insurance to guarantee your data projects get delivered and your stakeholders are satisfied during the whole process. Who doesn't like regular updates on the progress, not to mention the trust you'll build and the way this will help to advance your career?

I've done two complete house renovations. I loved inspecting the house whenever I could and receiving text messages from my contractors on the progress they'd made. It felt good to be involved every step of the way. Regular communication is especially important when a company's data analytics effort hasn't been successful, trust is low, and the silos between teams are wide. I'll let you in on a little secret – what I describe here is the norm in the industry. While online data influencers may paint you a career of a lifetime, it's usually filled with tight resources and impossible deadlines. You never have enough time to process much, yet you have to deliver.

Make Regular Communication a Habit

Data teams usually disappear whenever a project starts. Don't be one of those people. Set the tone for regular communication. Reach out and ask questions regularly. I know some of you might think, "Well, the business doesn't reach out to us…" However, you're not in elementary school anymore. This is a business environment, so reach out to them and get the job done or face the consequences of failed projects.

If you have no questions, demo progress and ask for feedback. Stakeholders love seeing progress; it makes them feel included. How often should I reach out to them? You should have at least a simple weekly IM or email update to the immediate stakeholders you're working with and a biweekly email for all stakeholders involved. Whenever you add a few new features, demo them and get their feedback. It doesn't have to be daily, though. If you do that, some people might find you annoying. Please use common sense.

Regular communication helps you build trust and credibility with your stakeholders. This way, you're always present and actively interacting with them. People will come to enjoy the routine you set up. Your stakeholders will know what to expect from you. Keep this up. This will be one of the best time investments in a project. The more you do it, the more efficient you'll become.

Types of Stakeholders

This isn't a comprehensive list of stakeholders. However, it serves as a guideline for you to understand how to communicate with them. It's worth mastering the art of communicating with them clearly and catering to their needs. It'll pay dividends. If you follow through consistently, you're going to become a data unicorn. Besides the consistent effort on regular communication, it's worth treating everyone as your most precious customer. The return on investment from this is unlimited. Not only will you enjoy your work better, but you'll also jump-start your career. And your stakeholders will get to experience a world-class stakeholder experience.

Business Project Leads

This is the most important type of stakeholder in your project. They'll be the best advocates for your team and you. You must develop a great relationship with them. They have a vision for the end users, the business, and a timeline for the project. Learn the business from them and work closely together. At the beginning of a project, you might want to have daily interactions with them. It's easier to meet regularly to ensure the technical requirements are correct. Once you pass that stage, you can dial it down to weekly progress updates.

Data Owners

Data owners are responsible for a particular source system. For example, they can be a Salesforce administrator, an SAP manager, or a controller. You need data owners to gain access to the data for your projects. They're often lifesavers when your stakeholders and you can't figure out why the results look weird or wrong. They'll be able to help you navigate complex data issues and the technical issues that a business project lead can't help you with. Depending on the source system they're in charge of, they might or might not know the business as well as your business project leads. However, it's always good to learn the business from anyone you can to enrich your understanding of the data and the business.

End Users

These are the people you often forget about, a habit which can also contribute to the failure of a data analytics project. It happened to me a few times. My business project lead and I would be working hard to make the dashboards look awesome and user-friendly. However, we forgot to find some beta users during the development stage. It's important to find opportunities to interact with potential end users at the beginning of a project. Although the business project lead is the go-to person, end users can often tell you things you missed. This is especially true in BI visualization tools. Pay close attention to their feedback. As important as it is to involve them in the process, they might be on the less technical side. Don't try to cater to all their suggestions. Pick a few good ones and implement them. Your business project lead is still the most important type of stakeholder.

Executives

It depends on the size of the company, but executives usually aren't your direct stakeholders. However, they'll know if you're doing a good job. Data touches every part of a company. There are lots of discussions behind the scenes on what value data analytics can deliver. Find out what your executives are worried about, either through an occasional one-on-one meeting with them or through your business project leads. You need to align your data analytics effort with their business strategies.

I know this kind of information isn't in your purview. That's why it helps to develop a good relationship with your business project leads. They'll share what your CEO wants them to do. Pay attention to these little cues. The next time you see your executive leaders, you can briefly mention what you learned from your business project leads and assure the data analytics effort is aligned with the business goals.

Junior Staff

You may never think about them, but they're just as important. You need as many supporters as possible for your data projects. You might wonder why I put so much emphasis on getting support and being seen. It goes back to the resource planning concept. At some point, everyone will become an end user of your data products. This is a resource everyone shares. You want to make sure that your company's money and time are well spent on your projects and get the most out of them. Since everyone can potentially be a user, you need to get to know them. You don't have to cater to everyone's preferences. However, you want to create the impression that you'll be there to help them when they need you.

Another reason to engage junior staff is that you never know who is ready to learn more. When they're interested in what you do, it makes it easier to find the next data owners and establish self-service analytics programs. If you only focus on interacting with your business project leads, it might be hard to roll out self-service programs. I find it satisfying to mentor the upcoming people to take my spot and do better than I can. It ensures that your company will always have talent ready to take on data analytics. It also ensures your projects are well received at all levels.

Team Members

Sometimes, your team members can be your stakeholders. For example, you might need a cloud architect to set up a development or a production environment, so you can take your projects to production. You might need a data pull that's only managed by the IT, not by any data analysts from the business. I often get annoyed by how slow some technical teams are. It drives me insane when I have to wait for five weeks to get access to a database without any updates on the progress. If you want to know how your stakeholders would like to be treated, you can start by thinking about how you'd like to be treated if you were them. If you don't like radio silence, you shouldn't do that to your stakeholders.

How Does Regular Communication Resolve Difficult Situations in Data Analytics?

Data analytics is a diverse field with unlimited challenges. I categorize all possible challenges into four types. I'll explain why regular communication is necessary to resolve these challenges. In the third part of this book, I'll focus on how to use regular communication to resolve these challenges. You'll have my step-by-step guides to navigate your daily work with your stakeholders.

Challenge One: Tight Timelines

When people want digital transformation, they want it yesterday. You might wonder what digital transformation means. I struggle with that too because, apparently, most leaders have a different definition of it. However, it's most often about how we access data and make good use of it for the business – among other things. Although we know how daunting this goal can be, it's always fast-paced, and no one seems to have any patience for it. I understand how hard development can be, because I was once a data engineer. It's hard to keep up with the demands. That's why it's crucial and necessary to have regular communication with your stakeholders. When your stakeholders trust you, they won't pester you about the little things, because they understand the challenges you face through regular communication. That way, if you have to ask for a little more time, it won't sound like an excuse because there is trust.

What you'll find is that most timelines are arbitrary. Your stakeholders don't have a good grasp of how long it'll take to complete a project. Meanwhile, you know that development is hard and any weird data hurdle can throw you off course and cause delays. Looking at this from both angles, it's hard to estimate how long a project will take to finish, period. However, it doesn't mean it can't be completed in a reasonable timeframe. I can't emphasize enough how important regular communication is. It's going to save you from unnecessary headaches, an explosive outcry for not delivering, and frustration turning into resentment and lack of trust.

Your stakeholders will have goals to meet in terms of financial quarters. It's best to finish a project within a quarter. What if you need more time than that? Break your project into smaller projects and deliver one in each quarter. In this way, instead of delivering nothing until two quarters later, you'll have something to show in each quarter. It's up to you to decide how you want to be perceived. You might argue that this is a continuous project, and it can't be broken into two parts. Well, the truth is that any big project can be turned into bite-size tasks. It's best that you do that. Otherwise, it's just overwhelming for anyone to take on. Do you really want to be in a place where you have nothing to show for six months? You get the point.

Chapter 5

Challenge Two: Lack of Collaboration

People talk about data silos. In reality, there are silos everywhere in companies, not just in data. Your stakeholders are used to working within their groups and not interacting with people outside their teams. It's common, and I also fall into the silo trap from time to time. I wouldn't place blame on anyone who is doing this or criticize the way that people don't do anything to improve it. It's just part of work life. However, you can break down the silos with regular communication.

Train people to get into the routine of sharing and talking about what they do. When they get used to doing it, it becomes easier to collaborate. It's best to start from the angle of encouragement rather than blame. When a company gets bigger, it's just a natural part of growth. You have the power to help them by being the point of contact for many groups. In fact, in order to succeed, you need to be the center of communication. If you want to increase the level of collaboration, it starts with you.

You don't need to wait for your manager to do it. You don't need to wait until your company starts Agile transformation. You can do this now by yourself. I promise you that people will want to join you. You'll not only deliver your project with ease over time but also stand out as a leader. It also improves the working environment for your colleagues. I enjoy getting to know people from different teams, even if they may never do anything related to data analytics, like people from the legal teams, and so on. We all work for the same company. Why not get to know each other a little bit? You have nothing to lose.

Challenge Three: Lack of Trust

If you think it's difficult enough to work in a place with no collaboration, things just get harder. Trust is like the air you breathe. Its absence is suffocating. Often, there's much debate about whether a company should spend time and resources on data analytics. If the groups already aren't working well together, the situation will only get worse. The temptation is to pick a side and support it. Don't do that. You don't have to decide who is most worthy of your attention. Nothing good can come out of it. Your goal is to unite everyone – or at least stay neutral so you can get things done. Hear each person out. What you'll find is that they never honestly express what they think or what they need from each other.

Back in my time in Medicare fraud detection, my manager and my director didn't get along. I had good relationships with them separately. One day, right before our big group meeting to talk about new fraud leads, my manager told me he wished the director would give him more time and resources to find new leads. And our team wasn't really pulling their weight, probably because the pay was too low. That same day, my director told me that he knew the pay was too low, and he understood that we just had to do our best with what we had.

Guess what happened in that meeting? My manager and my director started shouting at each other for not doing enough. About ten minutes into the shouting, I finally interrupted them and shared what they had separately told me the day before. They were able to calm down because of what I said. Although I didn't get to improve their relationship, I did get them to work together at an amicable level with me being their point of contact. They didn't like to talk to each other directly. Anyway, we were able to generate more fraud leads after that. This is an example of why you shouldn't pick a side. Could you imagine if I had? It'd only have made things worse.

Challenge Four: Difficulty in Defining Value and Scope

Most companies start data analytics programs without a strategy. For the last decade, many have struggled to monetize their costly data science programs. The marketing hype has just been unreal. How are you going to be valuable to your stakeholders? The answer is simple – by delivering exactly what they need. It can be making a dashboard, teaching them how to use Excel, automating reports via email, and maybe supplying a fancy data science model from time to time. People only demand to see value when you don't deliver what they need. Isn't that strange? You only need to focus on what they need you to deliver, not how to define value when you start a project. Value is different for everyone. Your CEO might be happy that the reporting system is getting automated by data teams. However, your CTO might want a robust data science program. You don't have to align their goals for them.

When you work on a project, get as much input from all key stakeholders as possible. Meet with them regularly, as the technical requirements might change over time. As they understand more about what data analytics can do for them, they'll be better at telling you what they need. This is common. Don't treat it as scope creep. Treat this as a sign of increasing trust. They want you to help them more. This is a good thing.

Define what they need and offer the best option to achieve that. You'll only need to be responsible for delivering the options you offer after understanding their problems and needs. Take one project at a time, especially if your company is new to data analytics. Value to them can be as simple as less manual work. However, bigger companies that have mastered the basic aspects of data analytics might want you to create robust models to predict sales and trends. The more experienced a company is in data analytics, the more complex a data project can become. Focus on what you can do to help them. The value will come naturally.

Through regular communication, you'll keep everyone in the loop with the progress and new features. People will have the chance to tell you what they need and what they'll need in the future. It's a great way to understand your users and adjust the course as required. If you don't talk to them regularly, you'll risk delivering the wrong product in the end. Please – just talk to your stakeholders often. It's such a waste of time and resources to deliver the wrong things. If you talk to them regularly, it's also impossible for them to blame you for not delivering because you'll have been listening all along.

Chapter 6

Core Competency Three – Equal Ownership

Data accuracy and regular communication can only get you through half of the journey to a successful project. You also need commitment from stakeholders involved and buy-ins.

People often believe that stakeholder relationships will just take care of themselves, and people will naturally assume ownership of a project related to them. No. You can't leave the success of a data project to chance. It's expensive and can have a tremendous impact on the business. You need to take control with intention and actively manage it.

What does equal ownership look like? Both the business and data teams need to feel equally invested in a project. This isn't between your business project leads and you. This is about commitment at the leadership level. A data analytics program isn't a pet project for the IT department or the marketing department. A data analytics program is something that will benefit everyone in a company. The senior leadership needs to feel equally responsible for such an effort.

What kind of relationship works when it's only one-sided? The same rule applies here. A data analytics project isn't just a project for a particular team. A data analytics project is everyone's project. Equal ownership encourages collaboration. I heard that one CDO willingly attached his bonus structure to the other team's collaboration with the data team, in order to produce optimal results. There is no need to make big gestures like that. Let's just stick to the simple things you can easily implement: it's always a good start just to be equally committed to owning a data project.

What can you do to facilitate equal ownership? It helps if data teams are embedded within the department that is the biggest consumer of data analytics or if they share budgets with another team. It depends on how your company manages resources for each team. No one size arrangement fits all. Just arrange budgets in ways that work for everyone and also facilitate collaborations.

Chapter 7

Core Competency Four – Equal Partnership

Now you understand it takes collaboration to successfully deliver a data project. They can't do this without you, and vice versa. It sounds simple. However, many people just don't get it. As well as equal ownership with senior management, your business project leads and any related stakeholders will also need to collaborate in equal partnership. This also means you appreciate their expert knowledge of data. I know some data people don't care about their stakeholders' expertise. However, that attitude is detrimental to the success of your project. There shouldn't be any us-versus-them mentality. Everyone needs to do this together.

Both parties should meet as often as necessary to get the technical requirements correct. There will be a few rounds of back and forth. This is normal, as data projects are complex, and the requirements often change. Be committed to making sure that everyone is on the same page. Don't let the idea of "scope creep" get into your head. This isn't software development, where you can ship a product and be done with minimal maintenance. Data analytics is a very business-driven field that involves a lot of people. It changes when business strategies change. You'll have to follow along with them and align with business goals. If you don't like this aspect of data analytics, that's something for you to think about in your career. If you truly dislike these kinds of dynamic uncertainties and having to talk to your stakeholders regularly, it might be best to stick to backend development or IT infrastructure, which are less customer-facing.

I've been in many conversations where data teams were fuming over something that could have been resolved by talking to the stakeholders first. They don't understand why they have to do so much even before the data is usable. Have you thought of raising your concerns with your stakeholders and asking for help? Your stakeholders don't just give you questionable data on purpose. Remember, they don't understand data like you do. They need you to help them understand so they can come up with a plan to improve. If a data project fails, it's everyone's fault.

Equal partnership is also your ticket to becoming unfirable in data analytics. Here are some questions for you to assess where you are right now. Are you a skilled partner or a skilled worker? What does this mean?

Let's go through the scenario below together. Imagine both Bob and Barry were Power BI developers at the same skill level. They worked for companies that were similar in size and structure. Let's see what happened to Bob first.

The marketing team wanted a dashboard that showed how well the marketing campaigns were doing for different business units. Bob only took notes during their first meeting. He didn't ask any questions. He suggested nothing, even though he had some good ideas. The team handed the data over. A few weeks later, he delivered a dashboard. He moved on to make dashboards for other teams.

He never talked to the marketing team again. The dashboard wasn't tailored to their needs because the interaction was one-sided. The marketing team felt the value provided wasn't good enough. Other teams felt the same way about Bob. They didn't feel like reaching out to him – because he didn't make himself available. A year later, when the company needed to cut costs, Bob was part of the cost reduction plan. He was a skilled worker but not a partner.

Now let's see what happened to Barry.

Barry showed up at the project kick-off meeting with intent. He took the time to listen to the marketing team's questions and concerns. He paused and described what they shared in his own words. At the end of the meeting, he understood what they liked and what the timeline was set for the project. He started making the dashboard and providing weekly updates.

During the week, he asked questions via IM or email. To get instant feedback, he initiated video meetings to demo new features. Whenever he noticed data quality issues, he shared them with the team immediately. The team appreciated the regular communication from Barry and asked for more feedback. Barry delivered a dashboard that was exactly what the team needed. How did he do it? Through regular communication!

He went on and built more dashboards for other teams. People loved working with Barry because he took the time to understand their needs. A year later when the company needed to cut costs, Barry wasn't part of the cost reduction, because he was an important partner for their data analytics needs.

Let's be honest. Are you Bob or Barry? Although this is an imaginary story, Bob and Barry are similar to real people like you. You can choose to be a skilled partner, not just a skilled worker. Technical skills are important, but only to an extent – because you work in the industry, not in academia. By now, you should have noticed that I didn't touch on any technical things you need in the field. As important as that is in your career progress, it's at its most important in the first 5-10 years of your career. Many aspire to do more than just producing dashboards and performing ad hoc analyses. Once you pass that junior role stage, you need to stand out as a leader with leadership skills.

In data analytics, it's important to be a partner and pool resources to provide business value with minimal cost and time. How do you take your career to the next level? You do this by choosing to be part of the value, not part of the cost. As you become a partner in all you do, work gets easier and better. Your career will spring forward. Choose to be a partner now. There is no time to lose. Engage with your stakeholders from day one. Take proactive actions to understand your stakeholders. You'll be surprised at the way a little extra work can take you further than expected.

Chapter 8

Core Competency Five – Trusted Advisor

A non-technical audience, your stakeholders, will always have a hard time articulating their needs. It's up to you to help them describe their problems and lead them in the right direction. You'll act as their therapist in these data analytics meetings. They'll be looking up to you for an answer. Take the time to help them formulate their ideas. Use Excel to help them visualize at the beginning stage. Please don't discount the utility of Excel. You can draft a simple dashboard look or a simple data science model in Excel. It's a great tool to ease your non-technical audience into more modern tools.

The business wants you to provide professional opinions. This is usually how it goes. They thought they needed a dashboard but didn't realize what they needed was actually an automated daily report via email. They might have thought all they needed was a data science project to start predicting sales volume. However, little did they know they had no IT infrastructure and cloud architecture to efficiently do this with.

It's your job to make them understand the pros and cons of different options so they can make an educated decision. Position yourself as their trusted advisor so you feel respected and heard. Take the time to listen and solidify their wants and needs into action. If you want to be an order taker, this isn't the project methodology book for you. The problem with being an order taker is that you fall into the cost-center trap, and you only do what you're told. Imagine carrying out what your stakeholders want, if they know nothing about data analytics and tools. Isn't it a recipe for disaster to take orders from people like that? I'm sure you've experienced this pain before.

Does this motivate you to speak up and proactively help them now? I hope it does.

Chapter 9

How Can Data Concierge Agile Make You a Data Unicorn?

Now you've learned the five core competencies of Data Concierge Agile. If you truly understand them, you'll become a data unicorn. This is something I learned from my manager in my first industry job after my time in academia. At the time I was in healthcare insurance, pricing Obamacare as an actuary. Each day we had an influx of data issues and had to find answers in a tight timeframe. The data discrepancy issues we faced came from the merging of several major databases acquired through mergers.

My manager was always able to find answers for the weirdest data issues. He had been a programmer before he became an actuary. However, that wasn't why he was good at data analytics. It was because of his "number" sense and intimate knowledge of healthcare data. Before people came to him, he usually already knew what was wrong with the data. Even when he didn't know, he was able to figure it out within a day. Nine years later, I'm in his position. I can finally understand how he was able to do it. With countless trials and errors, I've matured to his level. Here are the four telltale signs you're a unicorn in data analytics. It's also a way to see if you've mastered the five core competencies of Data Concierge Agile.

1. You Can Predict Data Issues

You've been in the trenches long enough to know when a data bomb is likely to hit you. Data can come from multiple sources. Different people have dealt with it, processed it, and even manipulated it. When you know the business, you can tell where it can go wrong.

As an actuary, whenever we had unusually high claims, the first thing I'd look for was possible billing code errors. For example, the revenue code in question was 111, but the data came in as 1l1, 1ll, and lll. This happened all the time. The data is always messy, but you've seen enough to know how to handle it with ease. I was able to correct that by using a SQL script in the backend before producing a final report for the business.

2. You Always Deliver What Is Needed

Take the time to listen to your stakeholders. Be a therapist for all their data issues. When they make a suggestion, you implement it. Although it sounds simple, you'll be shocked at how many stakeholders never get what they need.

During my time in consulting, our SQL programmer refused to make a change in the database schema because she didn't think we needed it. She was let go after we tried for months to get her to do it. That was when I picked up SQL – because I couldn't stand waiting for someone like that to stall my work.

3. Your Stakeholders and You Are in Sync

You understand the business so well that you know what your stakeholders need before they even ask. I was intimately familiar with healthcare data. I knew what my stakeholders wanted because I'd been a stakeholder once myself. One day I showed up at a kick-off meeting with a draft BI dashboard. After the demo, everyone just signed off, and I completed the project with minimal cosmetic updates.

4. There Aren't Weird Data Issues You Can't Solve

There will always be new data issues – even for the same things you've been working on for months. Someone might have updated the data without telling you. Maybe manual entries were not documented. Companies don't implement Git, a version control software, to govern their code base. I could go on and on for days. However, this doesn't scare you because you've had enough experience to resolve these issues. When a left join doesn't work, it prompts you to think of trailing spaces in the values that prevent it from joining correctly. With experience, you manage to figure out all kinds of data quirks.

What does it take to become a data unicorn? It's commonly believed that you need to know every cool thing in data science, machine learning, etc., but actually, you're a unicorn in data analytics when you understand the business and can speak the lingo. Technical skills are just a common denominator among the requirements for joining the field. It has little to do with how well you program in Python and your advanced understanding of statistics, although that does help. If you're not eliminating pain points for your stakeholders, you're useless to the business.

Data analytics isn't an academic function of the business. If you don't help the business bring in revenue, you'll become a cost center that can be eliminated. When you only focus on growing your technical skill set, it doesn't help you move up in the field. Data analytics is about helping the business monetize the data. If you can't do that, you should find out why and work towards that.

> *How do you know you're a unicorn in data analytics? You know the business so well that you're basically a stakeholder with fantastic technical skills.*

Part 3

The Seven Proven Steps to Implementing Data Concierge Agile

Now you know the five core competencies of Data Concierge Agile and how to become a data unicorn. What are the concrete steps to get there? This part of the book is guide-heavy. I'll walk you through actionable steps one by one. Data Concierge Agile implementation will require the following seven steps, in the correct order. You can go through step one to step seven however many times you need. However, it's important to abide by the order of these steps. It's not wise to listen to your stakeholder at the final stage of a project. You won't have enough time to correct any errors. Trust the process, and it'll work as intended.

1. Listen
2. Paraphrase
3. Find problems
4. Provide solutions
5. Communicate regularly
6. Demo in real time for feedback
7. Deliver exactly what stakeholders need

Chapter 10

Step One – Listen

Have you ever been to a therapy session? For those who've never been, here is how it goes in a general therapy session. Your therapist will ask you open-ended questions like "What brings you in today?" or "Why do you think you feel bad?" I know some of you are rolling your eyes now. Stay with me. A therapist's job is to help you find your answers. You're doing the same thing here, helping your stakeholders to verbalize their data problems. This is such a crucial step that you can't skip it. This is a necessary mindset for you to understand your "patients". If you don't know what pain they're experiencing, how do you even begin to "diagnose" them and add value?

Here are some possible reasons why a company starts a data analytics project. Leaders find their reporting process long and inefficient. Accountants find the reporting process exhausting because of the manual work. Marketing teams feel they don't have enough information to reach more customers. It always starts with a pain point. If people are comfortable with where they are, they won't need you. You need to find out exactly what they're going through by listening to them without bias. Once you know what problems they have, you can provide the right solutions for them to implement with you.

The biggest killer of a data project is poor communication. You can have the best team in the world. However, without communicating the value your team can bring to the table, you'll accomplish nothing. Without understanding what your stakeholders need to bring the business to the next level, you'll deliver nothing. As data professionals, you're probably not among the most people-oriented bunch. However, that shouldn't stop you from mindfully engaging with your stakeholders.

It doesn't require an extrovert to manage stakeholder relationships successfully. Trust me, you don't need frequent cocktail parties and long meetings together. I'm an introvert. As I said, in my free time, I read about economics and write sci-fi. I only have lunch with my friends once every three to four months. You get the picture. Some of you are probably more outgoing than me.

How do you communicate better and mindfully engage your stakeholders? It's not simply about nodding your head during a conversation or in a meeting. You need to embrace the therapist's mindset. Give them your full attention. Ask follow-up questions. People love to be heard. Sadly, modern society seems to deprive some of us of the most basic human needs – to be listened to and to be understood. Often listeners have formed assumptions before going into a conversation. For example, if you're really great at providing AI solutions, you might be tempted to give them AI-related solutions, no matter what their needs are. It's understandable but be aware of it.

I've been in enough meetings to see an engineer try to showcase their tech excellence by describing cool things they can build or talking about something unrelated to what stakeholders need. They don't spend the time to understand what they need. Although stakeholders sometimes don't spend the time to understand you, this book is focused on what you can do to help your stakeholders.

Stakeholders usually share what they need via email or maybe in an introduction call before this first meeting with data engineers or data teams. That's not enough information to start a project. You need to make sure they describe what they need in their own words in a meeting with you. This is a crucial step. If you get this part of a project wrong, everything else will be wrong. They might also want you to commit to a deadline. Don't do that until you fully understand what needs to be done.

Often, stakeholders believe they need machine learning models to explore the profitability of a product. It turns out they just need a dashboard to monitor sales. Sometimes, they downplay what they need. It turns out they need a complete cloud data architecture and an automated data pipeline for their dashboards. You won't know that until you listen to what they have to say.

It's almost guaranteed that they'll have a hard time articulating their needs. Here are some questions to ask them as prompts.

- What prevents you from doing your jobs and making important decisions?
- What kind of information is missing?
- If everything was possible, what kind of data tool would help you the most?

Through these open-ended questions, you'll get a clear picture of what needs to be done. It can either confirm what you learned from the introduction material or tell you something totally different. This sounds easy, but it's not often done. People have a way of rushing into things. It only takes about 30 minutes to get them talking and figure out what they need. This discovery conversation is crucial to the success of any project. Please don't skip this step. Just listen first. Remember the therapist's mindset.

Here is a common scenario to drive home the value of listening. The CEO of a company wants AI to be part of its digital transformation. The VP of data analytics wants to fulfill that vision for the CEO. You're tasked to make this happen. In the first meeting with them, all you hear are buzzwords in data analytics. There are no clear business strategies, and no monetization plans. It's up to you to ground them now unless you want to be measured against some fairytale metrics that will make you lose your job later because you can't deliver any tangible value to the business.

Implementing step one, listening to them as a therapist; this way you get to learn what the business problems are. The root cause, in the example above, is the fear of missing out. Guide them back to the core issues at hand. Start by getting them to talk about what people suffer from the most when it comes to data. Is it a slow and manual reporting process? Or is it a missed business opportunity: a failure to get new clients because they have no insights into the sales process? Explore whether or not they have a solid data architecture to support advanced analytics like AI. Explore whether they have the talents to perform this work. If so, how sustainable and how much value can come from this? I bet they never even thought of these things. Fortunately, you'll be there to listen and guide them.

I've been in these kinds of situations in the past without pushing back, and it caused me great pain. However, I was fortunate enough to make things work because I was skilled enough to deliver something they could use in a short time. Using Data Concierge Agile, I was able to establish trust among different groups of stakeholders and help them see that I was providing the best value for them and not just giving into the marketing hype. However, things would have been easier if stakeholders could just start with small incremental improvements before jumping to "AI" analytics.

Data analytics isn't just about getting insights. At its core, it's about resource planning. How can you do this most efficiently so they can improve the business outcome? Spend the time to listen. Stand your ground if they push you to agree with their unrealistic wants. They'll thank you later.

Chapter 11

Step Two – Paraphrase

Listening alone is not enough. You have to make it interactive. Once you listen to what they have to say, you get to describe their data problems and needs in your own words, which is paraphrasing level one. There are three levels of paraphrasing you'll learn in this chapter. It can be weird at first because you feel you're just repeating, not moving the conversation toward actions. It's okay to feel awkward at first because you're not used to doing this.

Why does paraphrasing matter? Can't you just listen, understand, and move on? Well, they need to know you understand! You need to verbally express that. Don't assume they know you understand. This is also a step to building trust. You must build trust with your stakeholders. When they trust you, it's easy to get answers and collaborate. It usually takes a few rounds of meetings to nail down the requirements for a project. However, it'll be time well spent because it's painful to deliver the wrong things, not to mention losing your stakeholders' trust. How exactly do you paraphrase? Let's look at each level of paraphrasing through examples.

Paraphrasing Level One

Have you ever felt lost in a meeting? I have. I've changed my career three times. I couldn't catch up fast enough with the new jargon that came with each transition. Stakeholders from different departments have their own jargon, making it harder to interact with them. Master paraphrasing now and never feel lost again.

It's a secret weapon that can be used to understand anyone from any background. I've engaged over 100 stakeholders from different fields and cultures. It works every time. How did I become an expert at paraphrasing? I paraphrased out of necessity when I first came to the United States as a poor international student. On the first day of college, I met a guy and had a nice conversation.

"See you later, Mo!" he said.

I thought, "OK, but he forgot to tell me when and where we'll see each other again." (Yes, I was that naïve.)

Quickly I learned that I didn't understand the cultural side of the language. It was difficult to make friends with the locals. I wouldn't allow anyone to end the conversation until I understood them. I'd bluntly ask what they really meant. In a way, I've always been a bit off socially.

People found it funny that I'd ask the most fundamental questions. If I didn't understand their answers, I'd repeat what they said to gauge their reactions. I started adding my own words to the mix as my English got better. Through my blunt etiquette, I made some great friends. Now I've become skilled at adjusting my speaking style to fit my audience.

If you want to master anything, start copying successful examples. If you want to understand your stakeholders, start repeating what they say. There's nothing to be embarrassed about. Think about this. It'll be more embarrassing later if they find out you just pretended to understand.

What do you do when you don't know much about your stakeholder's field? Practice paraphrasing. This happens a lot to me. Data touches every part of the company. I have to use data from credit risk agencies, Salesforce, SAP, etc. However, I manage not to sound like an idiot by only using paraphrasing level one. If I can do it, so can you. Here's an example.

> **Stakeholder Adam:** "We need to understand how this Medicare ruling affects our PMPM and how we can anticipate the experience in the coming quarters."

Now you repeat what he said because you have no idea what he just said.

> *Pro tips:*
> *Don't say, "I have a stupid question." Just repeat what they said right away if you have no clue. When people hear you repeat with confusion, they can't help but explain again without prompting.*

> **You:** "You're saying we need to understand how Medicare affects our PMPM and how we can deal with it in the coming quarters?"
>
> **Stakeholder Adam:** "Right. We need to understand that impact."

Start digging into the terms you don't understand.

> **You:** "What's PMPM? And why does this Medicare ruling matter?"
>
> **Stakeholder Adam:** "PMPM is per member per month. And the Medicare ruling prevents us from raising the premiums, even if it costs more to take care of our members."

Now repeat what he just told you and seek confirmation.

> **You:** "Per member per month is like how many members you have in a month? And that new law stops us from pricing according to the market's demand?"
>
> **Stakeholder Adam:** "Right. Any further questions?"

Do this one more time to make sure you get it.

> **You:** "Let me see if we're on the same page. We want to know how this new law affects our PMPM and see how we can adjust our premiums in the future."
>
> **Stakeholder Adam:** "Yes!"

Although you repeated 90% of his words, you're still moving the conversation forward. The flow of the conversation stops when you say, "Can I ask a stupid question?" Paraphrasing allows you to keep the conversation interactive and learn something. It makes it easier for your stakeholder to teach you without awkward questioning.

Here is a visual example of how paraphrasing works. Paraphrasing has three levels. You just learned level one. Imagine there are people on both sides of a bridge. The first level is to wave back at the people on the other side of a bridge by repeating what they say. The second level is to meet them in the middle of the bridge by describing what you hear in your own words. The third level is to cross the bridge and visit them on their side of the bridge by describing what you hear using their own words.

Paraphrasing Level Two

It's shocking how this skill is underrated. When people say you should communicate better, this is my version of it. When working with different stakeholders to build out their data analytics products, it's hard because they're from different departments, and they all have their jargon. You need to master paraphrasing and build instant trust. Now let's see how level two works. You're not only going to repeat things right away, but you're also going to add your own words into the mix. It flows a lot better than repeating 90% of the words. It makes people think you understand them, when you're just getting there, which helps build instant trust. Here is an example of how you can do this.

> **Stakeholder Barbara:** "We'd like to build this impressive dashboard that will lead to a better top line and bottom line. The dashboard will show our daily sales, what channel is making the sales, and the comparison between actual sales and our targets."

You don't know what a top line or bottom line is because you don't have a finance background. You don't even know what they're selling. However, you add your own words to make the conversation flow naturally.

> **You:** "I see. You'd like an awesome dashboard that will lead to a better top line and bottom line. It'll show your daily sales and winning channels in comparison to your set daily targets."
> **Stakeholder Barbara:** "Correct."
> **You:** "Could you give me an example of a better top line and bottom line? Also, what do your daily sales look like? What does a good-looking dashboard look like to you?"

What you ask here prompts her to describe the business in her own words. Encourage her to describe the concepts to you.

Stakeholder Barbara: "We sell shoes online. Our goal this year is to increase our margins by selling more expensive shoes. We sell about 1,000 pairs of shoes every day. A great dashboard will have a trend graph and bar charts showing our sales by channel. It'll be great if you can make it look pretty with our brand colors. Add more graphs that compare targets and actual sales."

Now you don't know what a margin is, and you still need more details. Stay calm and continue.

You: "About margins, how would you like to see that on the dashboard? And what is a good margin for you? I can envision the layout of your dashboard. Do you like everything on one page or do you want to only have focused graphs on one page and some nice-to-have graphs on the next?"

Stakeholder Barbara: "I envision the graph will show me margins for different categories of shoes, which are calculated as the total sale price minus the cost of the shoes divided by the total sale price, a percentage. I'm not sure what looks better – one page or multiple pages. How about you show me both, and then we can pick one?"

You: "Great, I have enough to get this going. I'll reach out when I have questions."

This conversation flows better than simply repeating the words. When you're more experienced in your field, it becomes easier to fill in the knowledge gap, and you don't have to rely on repeating their words. Now you know how to repeat and add your words into the mix. You're ready for the ultimate level of paraphrasing – using their words.

Paraphrasing Level Three

Let's take it to the highest level. This is like Goku going Super Saiyan in the cartoon *Dragon Ball*. Use their words when you paraphrase. Level three requires you to spend some time together with your stakeholders and observe what they like to say or care about in life. You can look people up on LinkedIn before meeting them. People write in a similar way to how they think. Just in case you're wondering, I look up everyone I meet online. It's a habit I picked up from doing fraud detection. It helps with paraphrasing level three. I'm able to match the speech pattern of my audience better because of this habit.

I'm also a direct talker. Corporate jargon isn't my strength. However, I sometimes have to use the speech style when talking to stakeholders who only respond well to that style. In the example below, at first, you might struggle a bit because you're trying to figure out their speech style. They'll respond well when you start using their words.

Chapter 11

Stakeholder Charles: "We're going full speed ahead with our data integration plans and digital transformation. It's an exciting time for us. I'd like all of us to wear multiple hats, and you'll be an essential part of this. Our goal this quarter is to integrate all our systems."

At this point, you have no idea what the data integration plans are and what "digital transformation" means in this context. What exactly do you need to do to deliver? Use what you've learned. First, repeat the part you hear, which is paraphrasing level one.

You: "I see. We're going at full speed with the integration plans and transformation. Thank you for sharing the goal for this quarter. I'd like to be part of it. How can we contribute to our goal by wearing multiple hats?"

Say what you hear first to show that you're listening and then dig deeper. Don't jump straight to the questions.

Stakeholder Charles: "We need to integrate data systems fast because our contractors need to be fully engaged. We'd like to be as efficient as possible. The CFO is excited to see our progress this quarter."

You need more information. Continue to probe.

> **You:** "You'd like us to work as fast and efficiently as possible so the CFO can see we achieve our goal this quarter. So how can we be part of it?"
>
> **Stakeholder Charles:** "I imagine we start gathering tech requirements from various stakeholders to start the data integrations and digital transformation."

Now you're still unclear on what to do. Then you remember Charles likes the phrase "economies of scale". To get him to explain what he wants you to do, you'll use that phrase.

Let's pause for a moment. You have two options now:

1. You can keep using your own words to get both of you on the same page.
2. You can make him feel like you're on his team by speaking his language.

I'll show examples side by side so you can see the difference and do what you prefer.

> **You (using your own words):** "You'd like us to work as fast as possible with minimal staff. The contractor is quite expensive, and the CFO wants us to be careful with the cost."

Now you get it. However, it sounds like you're just talking and bluntly explaining what he wants you to do. You don't sound like you're part of his team.

> **You (using his words):** "You'd like to achieve economies of scale in our digital transformation journey."

"Journey" is another word he loves from what you know about him.

> **Stakeholder Charles:** "Yes! I'd like us to be efficient teams and start working on it. I can see a team of three to four people on each of our data systems. We can do daily stand-up meetings with our contractors. Talk to Peter and Allen to get feedback on our system's specifications. They've been working with the contractors already. You can learn from what they do and apply it to your respective data systems."

People open up more when you use their words. It gets them talking, which is what you want so you can better understand them and collaborate better.

> **You (using your words):** "OK, I can talk to Peter and Allen to see how they work with the contractors and do that for my team."

You (using his words): "You'd like us to work in small teams and be as agile as possible. Learn from Peter and Allen."

"Agile" is another of his favorite words.

Charles is excited because you're matching his speech pattern. It's easy for him to respond to you. You'll still get to the bottom of the conversation if you choose to use your own words. He'll still respond to you, just not as warmly.

It takes time to understand and implement this level of paraphrasing. You know when you hit the right chord because people get more and more excited as they talk. It's not enough to just listen and get the ideas across. You need to make them feel they're heard and understood in their own words. If you're talking to an accountant, it makes them feel you're one of them when you use accounting terms like EBITA instead of company performance. This is what builds trust and induces collaboration. People love working with like-minded people. Even if you don't have an expert level understanding of the things they do, it can still do wonders when you use their words at a high level.

Let's get back to the visual example of the bridge. Repeating what they say is like waving back at them on the other side of the bridge. Using your own words is like meeting them in the middle of the bridge. The last level I just showed you here allows you to cross the bridge and visit their hometowns. I always love it when people don't mince their words and just say what they think. You can imagine how well I respond to outspoken people. The same goes for your stakeholders. The key is to learn to speak their lingo and match their speech patterns.

However, here is a word of caution on corporate jargon. I hate jargon. Corporate jargon is the worst kind of all jargon. It's one thing to match your stakeholder's speech pattern. It's another to be constantly subjected to it. Data Concierge Agile is the methodology to adopt for high stakeholder engagement. You should only cater to their speech pattern to an extent. If you want to have a better relationship with your stakeholders, start talking like an actual human being. Direct them away from corporate jargon. I've found that a lot of people just go along with others. If the loudest person or a leader loves corporate jargon, everyone follows along. Be a power of influence. Speak your mind with respect. People will follow suit.

Data projects are complex enough by themselves. The level of skills required to communicate well for a data project is harder than most projects. You don't want corporate jargon to ruin your effort to communicate clearly with your stakeholders. Here are some scenarios of what happens when corporate jargon strikes. I'll show some examples of it and what it takes for stakeholders to understand using Data Concierge Agile.

Scenario One – Data Project Kick-off Meetings:

Corporate Jargon:

"We're going to usher in digital transformation and innovate our data analytics function. In a few months, it'll reveal hidden insights to us. This project will improve both the top line and the bottom line. Data science will revamp how we work."

Data Concierge Agile:

"We'd like to understand your specific use cases before we provide solutions tailored to your needs. Could you walk us through a use case that you'd like to automate? Or could you share a business problem you'd like to solve using data?"

Scenario Two – Styles of Progress Report Meeting:

Corporate Jargon:

"In our Agile model, we'll do a system demo at the end of the Agile Progress Meeting. This progress needs to be scalable, so we can be on track to deliver continuously. The product manager and owner need to be there. We'll ensure that each team will be on track while gathering business owners' feedback between Agile Progress Meetings. Let's scope the vertical." (Seriously, what does this really mean?)

Data Concierge Agile:

"We'll meet as frequently as necessary to demo our progress. Now let's plan on a weekly schedule. Feel free to call me or IM me. Also, know that we'll have many questions regarding the data, and it'll be greatly appreciated if you or the data owner can make yourselves available. We're excited to deliver exactly what you need. The more we work together, the higher the quality of the end product is going to be." (Doesn't it sound more human now?)

Scenario Three – Final Delivery Meetings:

It's important to reiterate the business significance of the end product. Why did they need it? How does your work help them? Showcase that so they know you solved a big problem for them and didn't just produce some cool-looking platforms or models.

Corporate Jargon:

Well, they rarely deliver fully because they don't even know what customers want. They might present something, but it's usually half-baked. When asked why they didn't reach out when they had questions, they usually change topics. To avoid embarrassment, they might throw out tech jargon and constraints they ran into to show that you don't understand how hard it was. Again, why didn't they seek help before the final delivery?

Data Concierge Agile:

Successfully deliver what needs to be done exactly as their stakeholders need. Both parties have been in touch throughout. The final delivery is never a surprise. It's time to show off the good work.

Cater to your stakeholders through paraphrasing. However, stop doing this when the words lose their meaning, and make sure you can say what they want in plain language. This is how you implement step two, paraphrasing, using Data Concierge Agile.

Chapter 12

Step Three – Find Problems

Once everyone is on the same page after step one and step two, listen and paraphrase, you need to find the right problems to solve, help define them, and translate them into technical requirements. You might find it weird that you need the step "Find Problems". Didn't your stakeholders just tell you what problems they had? And you listened and understood them?

Let's go back to the therapist analogy again. When a patient tells you about his or her problems, it's about the symptoms, not the diagnosis. In this step, you'll officially diagnose your stakeholder's problems.

It isn't an easy step because you have to define the problems in a way they can understand (bedside manner), and yet keep the technical requirements for your team and you in the background. Meanwhile, this is such an important stage to show that you're an expert they can rely on. Imagine you're bipolar, and your therapist shares the bad news that you're officially bipolar. Now the therapist will instruct your family or the nurse on how to take care of you. These will be separate conversations. It's the same in data analytics. You let your stakeholders know what the real problems are (high-level explanation). You take that information back to your team to form a solution to solve that problem (technical requirements).

The problems they have will evolve with the business. You might need to go through step one to step three a few times in a project during the scoping stage. All the steps in Data Concierge Agile will take place in the order intended but will be iterative in style. It means that you'll go through step one to step six several times during a project to deliver the final product because of the messy data and change of strategies in most companies.

Remember that data analytics is about dealing with a living product. You'll learn to have the patience to build on iterative understanding, change of scope, and redefined value. I've engaged over 100 stakeholders, and I'll show you how to find the problems and win their trust. First, you need to understand the anatomy of the first meeting with stakeholders. This meeting is crucial. I treat it like a sales process where I need to close the deal on their trust in my team and me. The first meeting is not just a meet-and-greet, it's your first "date" with your business partners.

You must win their trust to establish collaboration as an equal partner, which is one of the core competencies of Data Concierge Agile. With the trust you gain, you can find their problems better and define them more clearly. I have mentioned the way that data professionals have the habit of becoming order takers. Don't fall into this trap. Ask them what the business context is. If they're not willing to answer, help them understand that the project can only be successful if you understand the business context. You want to be their strategic partner, not an order taker. A data project's success depends on both technical excellence and the business knowledge provided by stakeholders. Without that trust, you won't be able to collaborate efficiently and get the help you need.

There are four phases of the first meeting. In each phase, you need to complete certain tasks to establish yourself as an equal partner.

Phase One: Introductions

It's not the time to go off a tangent. Be on point and specific about what you can do for them. However, you don't have to go crazy with your credentials. They'll know who you are soon enough. Please also be mindful of not trying too hard to impress. Be yourself unless you're Chandler Bing from the sitcom *Friends*. Here are some dos and don'ts.

Dos:

Briefly introduce your team and yourself, literally a 30-second elevator pitch for each person. And your stakeholders should do the same. You must identify who the data owner or the subject-matter expert is so you can get help from them. These people will become your partners and perhaps mentors later in your career.

Don'ts:

Don't spend the whole first meeting on introductions and fail to find the right problems to solve.

Phase Two: Project Scoping

Implement the therapist's mindset here.

Dos:

Ask your stakeholders to describe in their own words what data functionality they'd like to achieve. Listen carefully, even if you've read the requirements in an email because sometimes it's wildly different from what they wrote.

If they can't describe it, ask them what is preventing them from doing their jobs and making business decisions in terms of data. Be a therapist for all their data issues. Let them complain about the data problems they face. Plan time to listen. Sometimes, they tell you in a form of a complaint. Pay attention to those. Those are usually the pain points you want to remove right away to increase trust and gain quick wins. I can't emphasize enough how important it is to listen first and find the problems together before jumping to the solutions. Your stakeholders often have a hard time explaining what they need. What are the chances they'll get it right in an email to you? Talk to them in person or through video meetings to understand first.

Chapter 12

Don'ts:

Don't jump right into the solution based on what you knew before the meeting. Don't plan out the whole thing for them without listening. You might miss some important requirements because of that. Don't deliver the wrong product. Listen first.

Phase Three: Show That You Understand Them

You need to use paraphrasing here. Remember we talked about the three levels of paraphrasing in step two. If you don't feel confident enough, just repeat what they say and slowly move up to using their own words.

Dos:

Describe the project in your own words, and let them process what you tell them. If you're familiar with their field of expertise, try to use the words they use, without excessive jargon.

For example, when I talk to technical people, I don't use the word "alignment". I just say, "Does it work with your schedule?"

When I talk to stakeholders, I say, "Does it align with your timeline?" You'd be surprised how well people respond to you when you use their words. Experiment a little and listen closely.

Don'ts:

Don't rush to finish the meeting and have no time for stakeholders to respond and react. You don't want to leave them confused. They need to know what they'll get from you.

Again, the first meeting is like a sales meeting. You need to close on two things – finding the right problems and building trust.

Phase Four: Ask Questions and Establish a Working Rhythm

It should be a given that you'll ask a lot of questions. Although you can ask them questions anytime during a project, this is the best time to ask most of the questions. Imagine asking them a fundamental question three weeks into a project. They might think you're incompetent. Also, set the tone for your working relationship. Let them know that they can always reach out to you. They can expect regular communication from you whether it's in the form of an email, a progress update meeting, or an IM in the chat.

Dos:

Ask all the questions you compiled before the meeting. You'll probably resolve a few while listening to them. Ask questions after you listen to what they say so you can ask great and specific questions, not just a lot of them. Let them know that you'll have regular meetings set up and will need help from them often.

Don'ts:

Don't ask a laundry list of questions without listening to your stakeholders first. This will make them wonder if you're competent and lose their engagement.

Now you know what needs to be done in the first meeting with your stakeholders. They'll trust you because you spend the time to listen, paraphrase, understand, and establish a collaborative rhythm with them.

Don't be surprised if the scope of a project changes. If you're in consulting, this part is usually well defined by the contract so you have the means to charge more or manage it without making anyone upset. However, if you're an employee, it's fair to say your projects never truly end because there will always be updates, adjustments, and modifications. It's part of the job, never a done deal.

You might find it particularly challenging to find the right problems when multiple stakeholders from different teams are involved because their goals aren't aligned. It's usually best to break their wish lists into several smaller projects to work on than lump them into one big project. Break the problems down into bite-size tasks so that your team and you can make good progress. At the beginning of the stakeholder engagement, it's important to show quick wins and offer value as soon as possible.

Here is a scenario to think about. You're tasked with building a cloud architecture and integrating various data source systems for Power BI dashboard development. In a normal situation, you'll first work on integrating data from different systems, building pipelines, and taking them into production before you make the Power BI dashboards for different business groups.

It sounds like a good plan, but in reality, it isn't. If you were to build everything sequentially, it'd take months before the business could see any value your data team can bring. Your credibility is basically in limbo. If they have planned for you to work on it for two to three quarters, that's great. However, this is rarely the case. They usually have an unrealistic timeline, and development usually takes longer than expected. Regular communication can help with adjusting the timeline, which I'll walk you through in step five. However, it can only do so temporarily until you have something to show. You should do everything in a parallel bite-size fashion.

Here is how you can do it that way without killing yourself. First, use whatever data they have – don't wait for the data pipeline to be ready – to make a draft dashboard in Power BI. If you have a team to help you, assign one of them to make a simple dashboard using the local files in the first week of the project. Showcase that to your stakeholders so they can get a feel of the end product in a prototype. Have that person continue to work with them to get the look and functionality right in the dashboards. Meanwhile, this buys you time to work on your cloud architecture, which can't be seen by your stakeholders, and it's difficult to develop. In this way, your stakeholders feel something tangible has been accomplished. And you can work on the hard technical stuff without losing their trust and engagement.

Now you've learned how to find the right problems through the therapist's mindset. It's time to move on to providing "treatment options" – provide solutions.

Chapter 13

Step Four – Provide Solutions

What you'll find is that your stakeholders are often not aligned in terms of timelines and goals. Different groups have different priorities. You mustn't take sides. If they're really out of alignment, you can ask them who should make the final decision and wait for that answer before providing options to solve the data problems they have.

If they're aligned, proceed to offer the solutions only after you have the time to think them over. It's never a good idea to provide solutions at the end of the first meeting. The solutions might be easy and obvious to you. However, it's best to wait a day or two. You need to make sure that you actually can deliver on time and have the resources to do so.

In the previous section, on the core competencies of Data Concierge Agile, you learned that you need to be a trusted advisor. Believe it or not, you have more power to help your stakeholders than you know. Don't let your stakeholders take the lead and go crazy on marketing hype. They'll value your professional assessment of their data issues. You'll encounter opposition. Sometimes, you might find yourself being the only opposing opinion. This happens to me a lot. I used to doubt myself. Why was I the only one with a different opinion? It's never fun to be in this kind of situation. However, I eventually learned that people are afraid of speaking their minds. Most people just go along with the loudest person in the room. Be brave. You're in charge of an expensive data project in a company. Make sure the money and resources are well spent!

It's important that you guide them with options and the right solutions. Don't just ask what they want. Give them limited options to choose from. Present them with two or three options instead of ten. Again, don't let them follow the marketing hype to do something that won't provide value to the business immediately. The same goes for you. Please think it through carefully when you do this. Are you doing this for their good or for your resume to look good? Many people in the field do resume-driven data analytics for fear of missing out. Remember, you're fulfilling the need of the business, not for your own upskilling. The upskilling will come naturally as you mature in the field.

Many times BI tools like Power BI will do just fine. However, some managers have to have Looker because it's of the "Modern Data Stack". What does that mean? Everything that isn't Excel is part of the "Modern Data Stack" to me. It's also worth considering reducing the number of tools you need to build a cloud architecture and an ETL process. If you're going for AWS, which is the most common route, you'll need dbt, Apache Airflow, Amazon Redshift, and many other things to get the pipeline orchestrated. Have you thought of using Azure Synapse, which can do all that data pipeline orchestration in one single platform? This is just an example. I'm not affiliated with any of the companies that sell these tools.

You'll guide them on everything from the choice of tools to the way a project is delivered. It's best to start with bite-size tasks and build up momentum from the get-go to gain visibility and credibility. Break down the big goal for data analytics efforts into smaller projects. Make sure that every key stakeholder agrees with the plan. Get them committed to providing expert knowledge on the data and answering your questions promptly. Make it clear so they can follow your lead.

A lot of companies like to use formal project management methodologies to run projects like this. I'm not against it. However, I like simple things. I know the terms stand-up, scrum, etc. in Agile are confusing to most stakeholders. If you must follow one of those project methodologies, keep those terms within your team. Don't confuse your stakeholders any further. Their job is to focus on helping you to make sense of the data, not following Agile. Through your interactions with them, they'll already experience the Agile working process, especially when you practice Data Concierge Agile. There is no point in burdening them with these terminologies.

Besides providing expert guidance, there is another emotional aspect you'll need to manage. Often your solutions become a threat to some stakeholders, especially anything with automation. What do you do when a coworker is threatened by data analytics initiatives? People are afraid of losing their jobs when you finish automating their work. They're worried that Power BI dashboards will replace them. It's a legitimate concern. They wonder what they would do with their extra time. Meanwhile, you're on a roll building one dashboard after another. And you wonder why they don't want to talk to you. Why aren't they as excited about the new enhancements as your CTO and you?

Your relationship with stakeholders can become competitive when people are afraid of your data initiatives. It's a battle between the new ways and the old ways. This is quite inevitable. This isn't the time to be the cool kids in town, but a leadership opportunity for you to form a collaborative community. Here is what you can do to prepare them for these new changes.

Present Yourself as a Partner

You're here to work side by side with your stakeholders. This isn't a hostile takeover. Their leaders understand the value of data analytics and want to help them use their time better. Here are some openings you can use when you work with them to set the tone. I also include examples that can trigger people unintentionally so you can see the difference yourself.

Dos:

"My team will help you free up your time and work smarter with less stress. Imagine getting things done faster and better in less time through our new data analytics initiatives."

"Wouldn't it be nice if you can just focus on what the data is telling you and not worry about how to get insights? That's why I'm here."

Don'ts:

"The leadership has set goals for us to automate anything possible. We need to get this done in the first quarter. Tell me where your data is."

"I can't believe how much time you spend on manual processes. Our new dashboard is going to change that."

Introduce the Changes Steadily

Some people will remain resistant. You need to speak gently but act firmly and consistently. Don't go to their managers and complain about it. This is your conversation and relationship with your stakeholders, not with their bosses. If they remain stand-offish, unwilling to help or provide data, you can have a private conversation on the side.

Dos:

"I've noticed some resistance from you. Could you help me understand why?"

You need to explore the root of their resistance, which is most likely fear. Again, the therapist's mindset applies here too. Your goal is to remove whatever is blocking them by showing you're here to help them.

Don'ts:

"My team is working really hard. When will the data be ready?"

Invite Them to Mentor You

It's not enough to have them warm up to you. You need to solidify this relationship. When work gets into a good rhythm, invite them to teach you about their work and share their expertise. Learn from them. I can't stop thinking about how much I've learned from my stakeholders, especially the non-technical ones. They often have deep knowledge of the business that helps you spot issues in the data. Positioning them as your mentors not only improves your relationships with them but also makes you even more valuable to your company than when you started. You'll be armed with both technical skills and domain knowledge. That's when you take data analytics to the next level and become a data unicorn.

Help Them Shift Focus to Strategic Work

Your value doesn't end here. Now it's your turn to make them more valuable to the company too. It's hard to shift the mindset from doing manual work for hours and hours every week to having less to do and more free time. You'll lead by example. Share how you use your downtime at work to learn new things in the field when a pipeline is running on auto-pilot mode. Show them how you delegate tasks to others and how you use that time to build relationships with them.

More Details on Different Types of Stakeholders

Next, I'd like to go into a bit more detail on how you can help different types of stakeholders through this transitional period. The following is not a comprehensive list, but it does capture the majority of stakeholders you'll encounter.

Technically Capable Stakeholders:

Tech-savvy stakeholders are the best, even though they're rare. I'd spend more time tutoring them on how to build simple things themselves, such as changing the dashboards' color and font, etc. They're usually interested in self-service types of projects. It's just incredible to work with stakeholders like this. They may become data unicorns faster than you can. It's always nice to see your students go places.

Senior Level Stakeholders:

These are leaders in various business units. Often, they're your business project leads. You'll want them to be your best advocates, and you can solidify this relationship by delivering the products they need. Work with them to break a big project down into bite-size tasks. It's not only easier to deliver but it also helps you to deliver better and faster.

Set up regular meetings with these leaders to share updates on all the small wins. When it's budget season, they'll vouch for your accomplishment and get you the resources you need. Help them understand that data analytics can lead your company to a better position to sell products. Most companies want to monetize their data but are clueless about how they can achieve that. Be a leader for them. Help them strategize through simple actions so they can take small wins and see results right away.

Entry Level Stakeholders:

Show them how automation saves time. When you're young and new at a company, you learn from what people are already doing. Sometimes, it's the old-fashioned way, like manual work in Excel. It's time to break that tradition and eliminate the generational knowledge gap. Introduce them to the data analytics capabilities your team can offer them. Help them to present impressive dashboards to their leaders. If, for instance, they're salespeople, help them to see that they'll get better results once they have more time to focus on the client relationships, and spend less time manually entering data.

You're going to act as a community leader for various groups by showing them why data analytics is good for them in their lines of work. It takes a "village" to deliver a data project. Involve everyone and be intentional about how you can help them.

Chapter 14

Step Five – Communicate Regularly

In the five core competency sections, you learned about how regular communication can solve the problems of tight timelines, lack of collaboration, lack of trust, and difficulty in defining value. Here are some detailed guidelines on how to do that.

Tight Timelines

I hope you don't ever face this kind of situation in your career. However, it happens more often than you'd like. Some stakeholders give you an ultimatum to finish a project before an impossible deadline. This happened to me a few times. I'll teach you how to deal with it and come out stronger and more valuable to your stakeholders.

Let's talk about why stakeholders feel the need to give an ultimatum. It usually all comes down to what happened before you came. They might have had problems in the past that were never resolved. Maybe the technical leaders didn't communicate as much as they should have or the contractors never delivered as requested. No matter what happened before, remember it's never personal towards you.

Now you understand it's not personal towards you, you can face them calmly. Let's walk through a pretend scenario together. Imagine the following conversation on the timeline.

> **The stakeholders:** "We'd like this to be done by the end of this month. We've been waiting for this project for over a year now."

Resist the urge to say "I can't do that" or "That's impossible." True, it's probably impossible. You'll tell them that soon, just not immediately. It's best not to use the word "impossible". When they're already upset, it triggers people. You can say it in the following way.

> **You:** "I see. You'd like this to be done by the end of this month. Usually, projects like this will take about two to three months with a solid team. Could you help me understand why you'd like it to be delivered in that timeframe?" (Say this in a neutral and calm tone.)
>
> **The stakeholders:** "Well, we started this project a year ago, and I've not received any updates from our data teams. If I don't have a deadline, I'm afraid nothing will happen."

Chapter 14

Usually, they'll express their frustration in full. Let them talk. If people on your team want to defend themselves, signal them to stand down. They can defend themselves by delivering value later. When the stakeholders are done talking, you paraphrase what you heard.

> **You:** "I hear you have received no updates about the data project, and you're frustrated and believe that this pattern will continue. That's why you think setting a tight timeline might make things move forward faster."

It's important to use "You" in your paraphrase. Don't say "The data team has not given you any updates on…" because your team may already be offended and stressed. Your goal is to gain the trust of the stakeholders and increase the morale of your team. You don't want to throw anyone under the bus, even if your team is at fault. What you say next is crucial to pacify both parties.

> **You:** "Now I understand where you're coming from. I'm fully committed to completing this project. Could we have weekly meetings for progress updates with you starting next week? I'll walk you through what my team has accomplished during the week, what needs to be done next week, and what help we need from you."

Usually, stakeholders will agree to this. If they press you to commit to the tight timeline again, here is what you say: "I'd really appreciate it if we could revisit that timeline weekly during our progress meetings."

Now you just tactfully avoid a meltdown from the stakeholders. Here are two things you MUST do to increase credibility and morale for your team going forward.

1. You MUST follow up and hold those weekly progress meetings. Make them short and sweet. Give them all the information, and the estimated timeline to complete parts of the project, and ask questions in these meetings or during the week. Some people like to cancel meetings at the last minute. It's disrespectful. Just show up and showcase the progress unless you get nothing done. If you get nothing done for whatever reason, explain yourself in these meetings. Or, if you must, you can cancel the meeting and explain in the email. This isn't optimal, but it might reduce the chance of yelling. Either way, you need to tell them what happens each week.

2. You MUST have a meeting with your team and communicate the following. Now they're upset. Regardless of whether it's their fault or not, your stakeholders should be the focus. If it took a year to get nothing done, as in this scenario, something was clearly wrong.

Here is what you say, "We'll work on the project as if we were committed to the original tight timeline without killing ourselves for now. We'll monitor our progress closely and ask questions as soon as we run into roadblocks."

If they're still mad at the stakeholders, let them be. In a few weeks, they'll feel better because the stakeholders will back off. Your weekly meetings will rebuild that trust between the data team and the business. Yes, it's stressful. However, you'll see your relationships with the stakeholders improve steadily. They'll know you're committed to delivering and will communicate with them regularly.

In a few weeks, they'll be able to work with you on a reasonable timeline to complete this project because they know what's going on and how much it'll take to deliver it from your weekly meetings! It never hurts to overcommunicate.

Lack of Trust

Have you ever dealt with cranky stakeholders? No matter what you do, they don't seem happy. In data analytics, communication is grossly overlooked. The lack of it hinders the whole stakeholder experience. It's hard enough to deal with data. Now you need to manage expectations from various teams. Everyone's definition of value is different. However, it doesn't have to be this way. The root cause of this attitude issue is lack of trust. You need to rebuild that.

Here are four ways to manage cranky stakeholders. Firstly, remember that it's not your fault. These stakeholders won't stay mean if you follow the tips below.

1. Don't Take It Personally

They had bad experiences before. This is more common than you think. A company decided to build its first BI dashboard or a data science project. Due to lack of experience and hiring complications, they went for a big-name consulting firm or some contractors.

Most of the time, it turns out badly. It's hard to find reliable contractors. Even big-name consulting firms drop the ball from time to time, not to mention how expensive it is. Now you're here to help them. They've been frustrated for a long time. It makes sense that they're impatient with you. Just respond calmly and stay professional. Listen to their needs. Nail down the technical requirements. Focus on what you can do now to make things right. Don't promise the sky. Make sure you break down a big project into digestible tasks to work on.

2. Acknowledge How They Feel

Although you don't take it personally, that doesn't mean things won't get worse. That frustration still needs to come out somehow. Be a therapist to their data needs. When they vent, don't deny their feelings. You must acknowledge those negative emotions. Ask them why they feel that way. Listen carefully. You'll hear some things that might not be true at all. Just don't take it too seriously. When people are upset, they'll say anything. This is the time you'll learn the things they need the most. As soon as you provide that, you're golden. It's instant credibility. Turn a crisis into an opportunity right there.

3. Reach a Middle Ground

Data analytics projects are complex. Sometimes, there are no good solutions to fix a long-term problem. For example, some companies want to integrate data from various source systems, but they don't have any data quality rules or processes in place. How do the data talk to each other reliably? How do you run a data science model on crappy data? Sigh. However, you can take baby steps to improve the situation.

Help them understand you're doing the best you can through listening and paraphrasing. These are the first two steps to implementing Data Concierge Agile. Find out what the most important thing is and solve that first. Don't come up with a giant plan for improvements. Break the big goal down into bite-size tasks. It seems like I've said this over and over again, but it needs to be said over and over again. I'm constantly in an overwhelming situation. For some time, I was in a team of one. I had to build pipelines to integrate data, build three Power BI dashboards, deal with vendors and contractors, and manage stakeholder expectations with regular meetings. I was the data engineer, data analyst, and data manager. It was unbearable, to say the least. I actually had to hire a career coach to get me through this dark time of my career. I was working over 100 hours per week.

How did I get my messed-up work situation back to a normal and acceptable degree? As well as hiring a career coach, what I did was to write down everything I needed to do on OneNote. I grouped them into task categories. I only worked on the most important things first. How do you know what the most important things are? Think about what will happen if you fail to do some of the things you need to do. Which ones would have the most catastrophic effect on your projects? That's how you know. For example, you could take your time to build a solid cloud architecture for a data science model because this will provide a great foundation for any future use cases. However, the business won't be able to feel any tangible difference for several months. You have to manage stakeholder expectations to succeed. If you don't, it'll get harder for them to trust you and help you because they won't believe you're competent.

You need to reach a middle ground with your stakeholders, given the limited time and resources you have. If they complain about not knowing what progress is being made, set up meetings or email them updates regularly. If they complain that contractors didn't understand what they needed, demo in real time with them. Have them show you what they need. Provide professional advice on how you can all achieve the tasks together. You won't succeed overnight; however, your stakeholders and you can celebrate small wins together.

4. Don't Compromise

Being a therapist to your stakeholders doesn't mean being a pushover. You're a data professional, and you know the life cycle of a data project. This isn't the time to give in to unreasonable requests. You acknowledge the problems and their feelings. Now it's time to demand equal partnership. Don't promise that a data project can be done in less than a month.

If they keep pressing on a timeline, invite them to weekly progress meetings. They'll feel the difference in the coming weeks and begin to trust you. I truly believe that very few people are unworkable, and I've been in many dicey situations. You'll come to find that people have usually just had bad experiences before you came along. Work with them, and you might turn your biggest adversary into your biggest supporter.

Another thing to keep in mind is that your stakeholders will follow your lead. When I was in consulting, the company's revenue model used billable hours. The consultants at my company loved it when the clients pushed for more manual work or urgent requests because it meant more money. Over time, it became unbearable for everyone at the consulting firm. However, it was too late to remodel that behavior back to normal business-hour requests because the revenues were tightly associated with those bloated hourly projects. When you keep taking your children to McDonald's, how easy will it be to make them eat vegetables? You already know the answer. Don't compromise on crazy hours and requests. It's never sustainable. With regular communication, you'll be able to modify stakeholders' behavior and rebuild trust.

Lack of Collaboration

The lack of collaboration is often due to a company's culture or size. As a company grows, it gets harder to get people together from different teams. Data analytics projects are one of the few times they need to come together.

The answer is quite straightforward. To remove barriers to collaboration, give your stakeholders what they need with the least amount of resources and time. However, many people seem to be missing the point. Go on LinkedIn, and look at the emphasis on learning new tools and technologies in data analytics. The emphasis should instead be on problem-solving within your specific sets of challenges and scenarios.

We all have limited time and resources. You have to compete for attention and resources to solve problems for different groups. Sometimes you might only be able to get a few people from some groups but not all of them. How do you maximize collaboration given limited resources, time, and energy? My focus here is on what you can do as a data professional. Since you're not a CEO or a business leader, you can't set goals to force people to work together. However, you can make their time together easier and more enjoyable. Here are some meeting tips when they're together in the same room.

1. Spoonfeed the Information in the First Three Minutes of a Meeting

People's attention span is about three minutes or less. When you're in management and have at least three or four meetings a day, you need a mental break. When you go to a meeting that has 20 slides, you just want to zone out. Every time you have a meeting, especially a cross-functional one, give your stakeholders exactly what they need to hear in the first three minutes of a meeting. Your progress meeting shouldn't be a burden. It should be a meeting with clarity about progress. Here is a potential scenario for your reference.

Dos:

"We're meeting our goals in Project A although data quality is an issue. We have a solution for it. The marketing team will help us with that. (Things are well. We have an issue, but we have a solution. Don't worry.)

Let's talk about how you like the dashboard we recently built for you. Does it meet your needs for X and Y? (Asking for feedback)

We need some help with Project B. Please help us with the execution of new business processes for cleaner data." (Actions for your stakeholders to take)

Don'ts:

"This dashboard is still in progress. We were really confused with the data points provided. The marketing team told us that the finance team would know the answer. However, the finance team hasn't got back to us yet. We're still trying to find out what to do with data quality. Do we have data quality measures in all departments? What if we don't have one? This is going to delay our effort. We need new business processes to hold the leaders accountable. Data literacy is a problem here. We need to give people more training on data."

The example in the Don'ts section is the most common way people conduct these progress meetings. Having been in so many of these, I want to throw up. It doesn't solve the problems when you just talk about them. You should state a problem with a potential solution and ask for help on that. Please give your stakeholders a break and present the relevant information succinctly.

What can you do to increase collaboration through regular communication? Give people what they need to know within the first three minutes of a meeting – on the first slide in a big font. And close the meeting with clear instructions to follow if you need their help. Easy instructions lead to easy implementations.

2. Dazzle Them with Real-Time Demos or Whatever You Can Visualize

You don't need to have an MBA to become a slide deck wizard and dazzle your stakeholders. If you don't know what to do with your slides, a picture per slide and keeping text to the minimum is always a good start! Unless you're doing an audit in real time, visuals are necessary for a presentation. No one wants to watch you reading off the slides and looking at spreadsheets in PowerPoint. I repeat. No one wants to watch you do that.

Most importantly, you should do a demo of your progress. They say a picture is worth a thousand words. I say a drafted BI dashboard is worth a bucketload of credibility and trust from your stakeholders. If you master ways to demo your data science model, you're a hot commodity. Here I'm going to break down how you do this to win your stakeholders' trust.

BI Dashboards:

This is the easiest one to showcase. Your stakeholders asked you to create a dashboard. You can show them where it's at, and the associated challenges in each step. They'll appreciate your real-time demos. Nothing beats seeing the prototypes. This is the time they get to test drive the tool they want. Ask them what they like about it and what's still missing. And deliver that! Make sure to let them know there might be some technical limitations, but you're committed to getting it as close as to their visions as possible.

The most common request I get is to make the dashboard look like their Excel charts. I know some of you are cringing now. Come on. People like Excel, and it's all about what they need. My last company used Tableau, which was a huge challenge when they asked us to make it like Excel. I was able to convince them to stick to the looks Tableau offers and automate a data dump for them. We reached a middle ground. My current company uses Power BI. Although it still needs some workarounds, it's much easier to do it in Power BI. People might argue that the dashboards should conform to the modern style. I used to believe that too. With experience, I realized that what matters is that your stakeholders use them. If Excel-like dashboards are what it takes to get them to use them and stop all the painful manual processes, so be it. I'm here to offer help. I couldn't care less about the styles as long as they're happy.

Data Science Projects:

Depending on the model you use, it can be hard to create any visuals. However, you can graphically show your data model. I know the urge you have is to jump straight into the model and discuss the pros and cons of the sampling, testing, etc. That's what we did in statistical genetics. It seemed that every meeting was about P-values, parameters, effect size, and so on.

Make it a business-focus presentation. Start with what a model does for the business. Don't tell them the P value is 0.00064. Share whether a model does what they need it to do, such as predicting sales volume, categorizing types of customers, etc. You don't have to go into the details of what type of linear regressions is best for higher R-square, etc. Throw that out of the window. You're talking to a non-technical audience. You need to explain things in plain English.

Make sure to explain that the model isn't perfect. Give them a few examples of how your model performs under specific conditions. You don't want them to have the impression that a model can produce an absolute answer because it can't, and it never will.

Here is an example. You want to predict sales of a group of customers using logistic regression based on what this group has purchased in the past, their demographics, and so on.

You can show the results of your model in a tabular format using

1. current existing data,
2. current existing data enriched with third-party vendor data to infer missing data points, and
3. third-party vendor data in your model first and comparing that to the results using currently existing data only.

In this way, your stakeholders understand that your model is just a tool to predict an outcome, not to provide an absolute answer. There are ways to improve the outcome, but it might be overfitting, which is manipulating the data to see what you want to see. With your visualized presentation of your model and your guidance, they can decide how to use the results to support their business decisions.

3. Finish Strong by Highlighting the Way Your Work Helps the Business

You need to remind them why you're working on this project. You might wonder why you need to do this, since they already wanted it. Well, priorities shift, and people are busy. It's necessary to remind them. Think about how you teach a child. You talk to a child in simple terms, use analogies, and explain a concept in several different ways. That's what your stakeholders are like. Their understanding of data analytics is like a child's understanding of the world. Don't use jargon in statistics. Explain how this result can increase revenue or solve whatever problems they care about.

How can you improve collaborations? As far as you can, make your presentations digestible and give your stakeholders a mental break. Easy information creates easy-going stakeholders. Make short and clear slides. Don't ramble. It pays to rehearse what you want to say a few times before your presentation. Think about how you'd like people to present information to you: just do that.

As you get to know your stakeholders better, you'll find some respond well to tables and numbers. Some like a PDF report. Some love a good slide deck. Take advantage of what you know about them and cater to that. You'll be a star data professional before you know it. Give stakeholders what they need, with the least amount of resources and time!

Difficulty in Defining Value and Scope

Not only will your stakeholders have a hard time defining what they want but they'll also struggle with defining the value you bring and the scope of work. In data analytics, it takes trust to make things work. You'll have to be patient with them. I like the therapist's mindset. They rely on you to help them and get them to collaborate with you. One of my favorite analogies to use in data analytics is home remodeling. I've hired contractors to remodel my whole house twice. I had no experience in construction, and I was no expert in home improvement. My contractors were my trusted advisors. It was hard to hire a trustworthy contractor who knew how to collaborate with me.

Since I didn't know anything about what they did, how did I know I was hiring the right contractors? Simple. I inspected my house regularly. The best contractors updated me regularly, let me inspect the house whenever I wanted, and asked for guidance when needed. What we do in data analytics is no different from home remodeling. Your stakeholders are like me in that scenario. Through this experience, I can now see things through their perspectives and help them, without sounding condescending. I learned a lot from my home remodeling contractors.

Your stakeholders won't come to you and say they have a hard time defining your value. It'll come in the form of complaints, lack of engagement, or worse, direct questioning of your value using rigid metrics. Here are a few examples so you can see how you can implement Data Concierge Agile to help them see the value you're bringing.

End User Complaints

No matter how good your product is, there's going to be a one-star review. That's just a fact of life. One of the end users once complained about how hard it was to use the Power BI dashboard my team built for lead generation. He wanted to export everything into Excel. I'm not against people doing that. I understand the need to do some checking and customizations in Excel. However, the dashboard refreshed every 12 hours, so that wouldn't be an ideal approach. He threatened to stop using the tool because it was "hurting" his chances of getting new clients. The situation continued to spiral downward. I was, however, able to deliver a world-class stakeholder experience by implementing Data Concierge Agile.

People who weren't involved in the development of a BI tool experience this type of frustration often. I understood where he was coming from, but also knew that my tool was designed well. What I needed to do was to listen to him first and help him to get on board with using this new tool.

I let him complain in full first in our meeting. Once he was done, I paraphrased what he had told me. I addressed each of his complaints slowly, because a non-technical audience usually has a hard time understanding you. Go slowly and have visuals ready if applicable. He immediately felt better and became less annoyed, because he knew I understood him. Here I implemented step one and step two of Data Concierge Agile – listen and paraphrase.

We moved on to step three "Find Problems" and step four "Provide Solutions". In this phase, we went through all his pain points one by one. I provided alternatives along the way. He was relieved at the end of our meeting. He felt heard. I resolved all the issues I could on the spot and promised to get back to him on the rest of them. In this particular case, I only used step one to step four because it wasn't a project. It was a situation where I needed to help an end user individually. However, you can implement Data Concierge Agile in this kind of scenario as well as project management. This mindset is good at resolving all problems stakeholders have.

CHAPTER 14

Use Analogies to Communicate Value and Scope

Use analogies whenever possible. This is how regular communication becomes powerful. You have the channel set up to explain things regularly to your stakeholders in a way they can understand. They're always aware of what's going on. If they know what's going on and always get help from you, do you think they'll have a hard time defining the value and scope of the project? No. Keep up the regular communication and communicate in simple terms.

Now I'm going to show what I mean by speaking in simple terms, using an example of how I explain what a database is. This is a very rudimentary question for any data professional. Everyone in data analytics should know what a database is. How do you explain it to someone who doesn't know what it is? Most of your stakeholders can't define it. This isn't just about non-technical stakeholders. Even people on your team might not be able to define it well. Don't take what you know for granted. You need to figure out their baseline understanding at the beginning of a project. Otherwise, it'll be a very painful experience for both parties.

My team and I were trying to figure out how to automate a data-pulling task. I wanted to know what type of database my stakeholders were using. To me, it was a matter of figuring out the database schema and the login information. Once we got that, we could automate this via Azure Data Factory in the cloud. Simple, or so I thought. To my surprise, the meeting didn't go well. The stakeholders couldn't understand what we were trying to help them with.

"Where does your data come from?" I asked.

They didn't seem to understand my question.

"How do you access the data when people need you to provide it? What database do you use?" I clarified.

"I get my data using Smartsheet," they said.

We spent almost 30 minutes going in circles. They were frustrated by my interrogation.

I finally asked, "When I say the word database, what does it mean to you?"

They couldn't answer it.

We ran out of time and accomplished nothing. However, that last question was a breakthrough – my audience didn't understand what a database is!

What could I have done differently? First, I'd gauge their understanding before jumping straight into a task! Here is how you can save yourself from the pain I went through. Start with a question like this.

> **You:** "Could you describe in your own words how you access your data?"
>
> **Stakeholder A:** "It's from a SQL database that the IT manages for us. Pete writes the SQL code for us to get the data."
>
> **Stakeholder B:** "I get everything from Smartsheet. It's neat because I can do everything without leaving Excel."

Stakeholder A knows what's going on in the background. This person knows what a SQL database is and who pulls the data for them. You can continue to get your technical requirements for a project from them.

Stakeholder B is clueless. This person only knows that somehow the data shows up in Excel. Now you need to take the time to explain what a database is. Here is one way you can explain it.

> **You:** "If data is like money, a database is like a bank account where each record is a ledger. You can pull data by ledger numbers. A database is a place where your data is organized in a table format."

I know this is a grossly simplified analogy. However, that's all they need to know. They don't need to know if it's a document database, a relational database, a cloud-dedicated SQL pool, or whatever. Speak in simple terms. If an analogy doesn't work, you can show them an example of a database. Let them absorb what you just taught them. Encourage them to teach you what they just learned from you. Assess their understanding fully before getting the technical requirements.

You may find it exhausting because it is. However, it's worth the extra time. Yes, it's extra work. However, it's well worth the investment for better relationships with your stakeholders. It builds trust, and that will increase collaboration. Otherwise, they'll only see you as a skilled worker, not an equal partner. In the beginning, you'll spend a lot of time doing this. I promise you'll soon see the results. Your stakeholders will become more receptive to what you say because you aren't judging them. You're simply there for them.

Data analytics teams often become cost centers because they don't speak the business language. If you don't communicate your value to them regularly, how will they know you can be a valuable partner? Keep it simple. Use analogies when working with a non-technical audience. This is the best way to demonstrate your value to them.

Why Are We Obsessed Over Useless KPIs and ROIs in Data Analytics?

It's been a constant struggle to manage non-technical executives with strong technical opinions. "Let's track our productivity by how many dashboards our data teams can produce this year," they said.

Some track the success of a dashboard or a data science project by how many decisions were made based on it. Can you see the ramifications of this stupid approach? People work towards rewards. What if making more decisions using a data tool doesn't increase revenue? What are you going to do then?

These activity-driven metrics can't show the true value of data teams. The issue here is you're measuring the wrong things, not that data professionals shouldn't be held accountable for their products. So how do you measure the value of your data teams? The solution is a lot simpler than you think. Take the checkpoint approach. Go straight to the source – talk to your stakeholders. Ask your stakeholders how they've benefited from the products your data teams produced.

- Have the data teams asked for feedback?
- Have they delivered the things you need?
- Are they prompt to respond to you?
- Have they helped you along the way, figuring out what's necessary for your projects to make things happen?

People might be put off by this human approach and consider it an unscalable one, wanting to go back to the useless metrics. Again, when do you ever go to a meeting where people are counting how many decisions they make based on a data product? This is just an example, but you get the point. If you've ever been to a meeting like that, I feel bad for you because there is no win from working with a group like that. If you want to know who truly provides value to the business, you should go to the people they serve and find out. The true winners in this field are the people who know how to package all business value into the final deliverables.

The metrics issue is also an emotion-driven phenomenon. It's as if people are afraid of living by the principle of things, using their judgment. They desire a rigid framework to frame their success, eliminating all possible errors. However, even if you beat all the metrics, that doesn't mean you're good at your job – because it's just a checklist. People can participate in meetings, actively answering and listening.

That doesn't make them competent until they deliver something. Similarly, your data team can produce 10 crappy dashboards instead of one high-quality one.

Let's think about this obsession even more deeply. If someone asks you to justify your value, you've already lost. Why would they ask in the first place? It's because they already don't value your contribution, and they're trying to justify their assessment through your answers. It's a trick question. Here is what you need to do to get to the bottom of this.

- Where did the trust and connections disappear?
- Was it from lack of regular communication?
- Was it from a lack of engagement with your stakeholders?
- Have you been regularly asking for feedback?

Who can broadcast your value more loudly than some useless metrics? Your stakeholders and end users. Let them vouch for you. Build strong relationships with them and gain their trust so you'll never need to prove your worth again! That's what matters.

Chapter 15

Step Six – Demo in Real Time for Feedback

How do you get feedback from stakeholders? Do a demo with them in real time in a meeting. What does this mean? You showcase your work in front of them, preferably regularly. You might think it's funny that I have to paraphrase this. However, I've suggested this solution to many data professionals when they run into issues with stakeholders. They don't seem to understand me. They'd rather suffer through the back-and-forth emails than deal with the problems head-on.

I guess I'll never understand why people want to overcomplicate their lives. However, I'm only here to support you. It's up to you to make that decision. This is my tried-and-tested method. I see real-time demos as my secret weapon (along with paraphrasing). Here are three possible scenarios. I'll walk you through how you can do real-time demos for feedback.

Business Analytic Dashboards:

Get your draft dashboards ready and showcase them to stakeholders as soon as possible after the kick-off project meeting. This will increase trust upfront and eliminate unnecessary anxiety and questions from them. Through screen sharing or in-person meetings, encourage them to tell you what changes they'd like to make and give you instant feedback.

It can be intimidating at first. You may be slow. However, this is the most efficient way to get to the most tailored dashboards. You can practice it with your manager or a colleague first. Don't get involved in back-and-forth emails and cryptic suggestions. Stop doing subpar implementations. It'll solve most of your problems if you just ask them in person.

Data Science Projects:

It's still possible to do a real-time demo even if there are no visuals involved. After gathering sufficient technical requirements to work with, build a draft model with the necessary data loaded and get a few scenarios tested. Do this as soon as possible and bring your draft model to your stakeholders. Showcase the rudimentary results with them in real time. Walk them through what you're doing at a high level. If you need to, you can even build a mini version of your model in Excel to explain better, so they don't have to stare at the command prompt or whatever coding platform you're using. Help them understand how you can adjust the model to answer their business questions. Remember to pause and listen to their questions. Always answer in simple terms. Here is an example of what you should and shouldn't do.

Dos:

"Our model gives us the green light that our data can be used to predict XYZ with 50% confidence. I'd like your assessment based on your experience and your help to evaluate this model with me."

Don'ts:

"The P value of this regression model isn't less than 0.05 or less than its adjusted threshold. Therefore, we can't reject the null hypothesis. Please tell me what kind of accuracy you're looking for."

Seriously, explain in plain English. Practice doing that. It took me a while to get it, but it's worth the time! Decide on the details of the model specifications together. Show them how their decisions impact the models.

Ad-Hoc Requests Involving SQL:

If your stakeholders don't know what kind of data they're looking for, it's a great chance to write real-time SQL queries with them. In software development, this is called paired programming. Usually, you do this with a fellow programmer. However, in your case, you'll do this with your stakeholders. You might wonder if this will confuse them. It won't – unless you talk in jargon. The scenario is simple. They ask you a business question. You write a query to answer that question. Here is an example in which a stakeholder would like to know how many members were lost in the health plans because of a Medicare rule change. The analyst now responds.

Dos:

"Let's find out how many members we lost because of the new Medicare rule. First, I'll find out how many members we have in each of the Medicare plans by counting members grouped by plan IDs…"

Don'ts:

"I'm going to select column plan IDs and then just count months by plan IDs. This is the column I use to group it. Wow, it gives me so many rows of data. Maybe I need to join another table. What kind of table is that? Wait, I used the wrong table. What years are you interested in again? What's the plan IDs range…?"

Again, it might be intimidating to program and demo in real time. Especially in the beginning, you might sound like an idiot. I've been there. The example of Don'ts above could have been me at one point. It takes practice to get better.

However, I live for efficiency. Back-and-forth email threads aren't worth the time. Practice direct and real-time communication now. Stop hiding behind the email threads. Pick up the phone and call them. Do video meetings. You'll enjoy stronger relationships with your stakeholders because

Chapter 15

they'll know you give them exactly what they need, rather than hiding behind your data tools. You'll become an equal partner, not just a skilled employee.

Chapter 16

Step Seven – Deliver Exactly What Stakeholders Need

You've learned six out of the seven steps of Data Concierge Agile. I'm proud that you've made it to this part of the book. Now you'll learn the last step of my dead-simple methodology. I can't wait for you to practice these principles yourself. You're going to feel the difference.

How do you deliver what your stakeholders need? This is a burning question for many people. The answer is simple – just ask them! On Twitter, I came across a lengthy thread about how they could measure the value of a data analytics project. This group agreed on a complicated system to calculate the "happiness index" of their stakeholders. In that thread, no one mentioned the approach of direct communication. How do you know if your leaders are happy with your data teams and the value you provide? Just ask them. They won't bite. You'll run into two types of stakeholders. Learn to listen to feedback with a neutral attitude. Don't react to it on the spot. Just listen.

Honest Stakeholders

They're completely honest with you. This is the best scenario, even if the feedback is negative – because you know where you stand. Although it's no fun to be on the receiving side of negative feedback, it's definitely better than a meltdown later on, leaving you no time to correct any issues.

Sugar-Coating Stakeholders

They're too nice to tell you what is wrong, although this rarely happens in my experience. People are quick to complain when they don't have the data they need. If they don't give feedback, ask them what data issues they face at work. That way, you'll know if your teams or you have provided enough support and value to them.

The Importance of Regular Meetings

It's crucial to have regular meetings when you deliver data projects. Agile methodologies are at the heart of software engineering development cycles. Most of them have a strong focus on regular communication, such as stand-up meetings, product demos, etc.

The data field has recently followed suit, although not as comprehensively as the software engineering field; regular communication is still key. Using my favorite analogy again, a data project is like a home remodeling project. Can you imagine if your contractor just stopped talking to you as soon as the project started? And you wouldn't be able to see the progress until it was done. Imagine all the things that could go wrong!

Have regular meetings on your progress. Keep your stakeholders in the loop. Ask them to provide feedback. If there isn't much progress, replace a meeting with an update email or an IM instead. Never stop communicating with your stakeholders.

Don't let poor communication kill your good data projects. The more you communicate, the more likely you are to provide value to them. I know it's extra work. However, it's the best insurance for your projects, which protects you from delivering the wrong products. This last step in Data Concierge Agile is also the easiest. If you've been religiously implementing step one to step six, you should have very little to worry about. You know you're delivering what they need. The final delivery will thus never be a surprise.

Chapter 17

Time to Scale Up

Congratulations! You've learned how to implement Data Concierge Agile. I hope you already feel the difference. This is just the beginning of your journey to great data project management and projects of larger scales. You need to scale with the projects and company with the right teams.

Empower Your Company with the Right Data Team

Do you have the right data team to support your data analytics needs? For most companies, it's unnecessary to build a large team like the ones at Meta or Netflix. In the current business climate, having such a sizable data team is probably a thing of the past. With new tools like PaaS (Platform as a Service), more and more processes will be automated.

This means we'll have smaller data analytics teams in the future. The focus thus shifts towards understanding the business rather than just the technologies. Improved tools isn't the only factor that will make data teams smaller in the future. Companies continue to team up with companies like HCL and Infosys to provide their technical needs. It's more important than ever that you become a Data Concierge for your company. What's a Data Concierge again? Someone who is intimately familiar with technologies and the business, and who serves as a point of contact between data teams and stakeholders. Your technical skills might be outsourced. However, it's hard to outsource business acumen. That's something for you to think about. You should focus on business problems. The rest will then fall into place.

Although the following is about data strategies for data leaders, it'd be beneficial for all of you to think through it. One day you'll become a leader in the field and will need to manage time and resources for your company. So this section is important for everyone.

Business Problems

You don't need to be a data genius to know what business problems you need to solve. Start with these simple questions:

- What reporting process is manual and error-prone?
- What area of the business are you most concerned about? (Is it sales, customer service, etc?)
- How much budget do you have?
- How fast do you want to position the business better?

You might be tempted to hire a data strategist now. You can, but you should probably wait until you have answers to the questions above. No one knows your business better than you do. First, it's time to dig deeper and consult with your teams internally.

First Hire

Now you've figured out your data problems at a high level, you need to bring in an experienced business analyst with strong communication skills and technical skills, leaning heavily on communication. This is the role I call "Data Concierge".

Wait, why not start with a Chief Data Officer? No. At the beginning of your data analytics journey, you need someone close to the groundwork first. A Chief Data Officer might be great when you're mature enough to scale. However, at the beginning of the data analytics journey, you need a scout who is capable of many things. It's smart to start small. Unless a Chief Data Officer is willing to do the groundwork, I wouldn't recommend it.

The reality is that most companies don't understand what they need at the beginning of their data analytics journey. If you don't work with data, it's impossible to gauge how hard something you need might be delivered. By starting small, you can afford the time to study what use cases will give you the most value. Also, you need to consider how the leaders react to this initiative. Some welcome automation. Some don't. Data analytics initiatives imply that manual work isn't appreciated, and that's why you're looking for an expert in data analytics to change things up. You're not satisfied with the current state of insights you get from them.

It's best to bring this up as a solution, a way to remove their pain points. Ease them through the transition. Remember, this isn't an initiative to eliminate headcount. Although it sometimes comes to that, it's never the end goal.

Team Structure

It's important not to burn out your Data Concierge, your first hire. It's a lot of work to scope out what a company needs, especially when you have various legacy systems for your data. As soon as you have a clear definition of your first few use cases, it's time to hire a backend developer to help your Data Concierge process data and deliver projects.

For a mid-size to large company (apart from those huge tech companies), add a few more BI analysts and data engineers so your Data Concierge can focus on engaging stakeholders from various teams and building trust. They can also lead this small data analytics team.

Deliver Your First Use Case

Now you officially have a data team with the bare minimum data analytics functions. The first use case should be strong marketing to mobilize the rest of the company. They should clearly see the value in this. It'll get easier to collect more use cases from them. This is also the stage to get strategic. Not all use cases have an impact on the top line. The leadership team should decide this together. Again, the data team you have at this stage is still new. It'll get better as you go through more rounds of deliverables.

Scale Up

Imagine this. It's been about a year, and a few successful products have been delivered by the data team. Depending on the companies, you'll probably fall into one of these two categories when it comes to scaling up.

Data Analytics as Decision Support (Internal)

The purpose of data analytics has always been to reduce manual work and increase transparency in your processes within different business units. That is, your data analytics teams are used for decision support. You can build up the team by promoting from within if the right people with talent are present and ready to work towards it. Your first hire, the Data Concierge, can easily manage bigger teams and take care of more data analytics needs across different groups. On top of that, they can provide strategic solutions to mature the teams and stakeholder needs.

Data Analytics as Product Monetization (External)

If your company has moved beyond using data analytics as decision support, you might need an experienced leader with a great track record who can take data products to market. This leader will need to lead a larger team that builds out user platforms for subscriptions, sells data to a third party, and has experience in leading software engineers at a production level. If you're not ready to commit long-term, you can always hire a fractional CTO or a fractional CDO (Chief Data Officer) to work with you. At this point, the whole strategy of the company has changed as well, moving from selling products to data services. Maybe the CEO or the CMO (Chief Marketing Officer) can work closely with your Data Concierge until they're ready to take on this task – or until you find a right fit. It's always best to promote from within. It does wonders for morale.

Common Pitfalls

It's hard to set up the first data analytics program, no matter what level you're at and what size an organization is. These pitfalls are closely related to how the companies fail to scale according to their needs. There might be constraints on resources, timing, etc. Do your best, and just be aware of these potential pitfalls.

Understaffing

Please have at least two people to start your data analytics journey. It takes, at a bare minimum, one Data Concierge who can communicate and understand business use cases like a pro and one very technical person to perform the ETL and data warehousing work. You don't want them to burn out. This is going to be a long-term effort.

Relying Too Heavily on One Person

Somehow, even with multiple team members, the business sometimes relies heavily on the team member who can communicate the best. It's hard to even out the work and train up others at the same time, which leads to the next pitfall. That's why Data Concierge Agile has such a heavy emphasis on involving different types of stakeholders and training them so your company will never run out of talent.

Not Training Internal Staff

It's wise and efficient to train stakeholders who are already technically savvy. One of the financial analysts on the other team at my company was interested in learning Azure Synapse/ETL from me. I always welcome such individuals. This is one of many ways to scale up, and possibly the most efficient way. You don't always have to hire more people. Sometimes, a great team of contractors can work wonders, too. It's always best to start small and look around to see what resources and talent you already have.

Are You Ready for Your Data Analytics Journey?

Now you know it's not a one-team-fits-all situation. Your team evolves. Your data team will be perfected as you go through the stages in data analytics. It heavily depends on the context of your business.

Here is your data analytics journey map again:

- Find business problems to solve
- Get your first hire, a Data Concierge
- Set up a team, starting small
- Deliver your first use case
- Scale up according to the business needs
- Data analytics as decision support: promote from within
- Data analytics as product monetization: promote from within or find a go-to-market expert for data products

Avoid common pitfalls:

- Not adding more staff as you mature
- Relying too much on one person
- Not training internal staff to mature with data analytics functions

Chapter 18

What Is Stakeholder-Driven Data Analytics?

Data Concierge Agile has a laser focus on stakeholders. Do you often think through the lens of your stakeholders? No matter what role you get hired for in data analytics, you have to focus on solving business problems first, not scientific theories. Most data science projects have no clear monetization goals. The value they provide is often in limbo. The marketing hype continues in data science, just under a different name – AI or Machine Learning.

It doesn't matter what tools you use to solve your stakeholders' problems as long as your solutions are based on sound engineering principles and don't introduce more manual work. Be useful to your stakeholders. It doesn't help them if you're just trying to look cool. People often complain about the business failing to understand data analytics. Let me ask you this – do you explain yourself well? Be honest. How many data professionals do you know who are excellent communicators? I think you know the answer. On top of that, using your broken communication skills, you try to sell your stakeholders some "data science" solutions to a problem they can't even define without professional help. What good can come from that? Instead of jumping from zero to AI, here are the four stages of a stakeholder-driven data analytics journey to help you understand how stakeholders will collaborate with you.

1. Provide Information That Wasn't Available Before

The business has legacy systems, and it's hard to integrate data from different source systems. With modern cloud architecture, whether it be hybrid or 100%, for the first time the business can do cross-department reporting, enjoy automation, and eliminate hours of manual work. This is an infrastructure upgrade, a necessary first step.

2. Guide Interpretation of Data Results with Stakeholders

Once you've transitioned the company to the 21st century, you get to spend more time interpreting the data with your stakeholders. They start to think more strategically about what they want to do with their data. You're there to coach them and come up with valuable use cases that you couldn't explore before. This is the period when you solidify your relationship with them. Be intentional and strategic. Implement Data Concierge Agile step one to step six: listen, paraphrase, find problems, provide solutions, communicate regularly, and demo in real time for feedback. Be patient with this iterative progress and celebrate small wins.

3. Use Insights to Monetize

After a few successful use cases, as you're getting beyond just reporting functions, it's time to focus on monetization. Now the business has got a taste of what successful data analytics looks like, you can create products or tools to help increase sales or save costs. For instance, you can predict the seasonality of sales, the margins of each factory production, etc. There are endless ways to gain insights. You can even sell your data to other companies, if you have enough data volume in your niche.

4. Collaborate to Scale Up

Continue to collaborate with different teams, help people reduce manual work, provide insights, and train staff to achieve self-service. It's only a matter of time before they learn and join your effort. Your company will become truly data-driven at this stage. If you can focus on what the current data pain points are, you'll be successful at providing good solutions, and evolve to this stage.

Chapter 19

Data Concierge Agile Review

In conclusion, let's review the five core competencies of Data Concierge Agile.

1. Data accuracy
2. Regular communication
3. Equal ownership
4. Equal partnership
5. Trusted advisor

Here are the seven proven steps to implementing Data Concierge Agile.

1. Listen
2. Paraphrase
3. Find problems
4. Provide solutions
5. Communicate regularly
6. Demo in real time for feedback

7. Deliver exactly what stakeholders need

Here you go again – five core competencies and seven proven steps to implementing Data Concierge Agile in your data analytics projects. Your goal is to deliver a world-class stakeholder experience in data analytics.

No jargon. No ceremonies. You only implement what works. This is a playbook to help you get results. I hope you get to implement these principles and have a fulfilling career. I'll see you on LinkedIn or Twitter, my fellow Data Concierges. I'd love you to join my newsletter here, https://dataconcierge.co and claim the free gift I made for you.

Acknowledgments

I'd like to express my sincere appreciation to the individuals whose invaluable contributions made this book possible.

I'm deeply grateful for Jon Brosio, although we've never met, for his inspiration on Medium, which was essential to the success of this project. His ideas on how to create content and write online were truly the beginning of my writing career.

Special thanks are extended to Self-Publishing School, especially Coach Andrew Biernat, for his knowledge and coaching, which played a vital role in making this book a reality. His support and industry knowledge greatly facilitated the completion of this book.

I also extend my appreciation to Andria Gillis for her coaching, which was instrumental in finding my true passion – writing. Her support made a significant contribution to the completion of this project.

Foremost, I'm grateful for all the unpleasant work experiences and a series of career changes I had, which turned out to be the fuel for my writing process. It provided critical insights and direction that greatly enriched the content of this book.

Lastly, I'd like to thank Randy Bean for his support and wonderful foreword. His encouragement was invaluable and contributed greatly to keeping me going.

To all those who have supported me throughout this endeavor, your contributions have been instrumental in the realization of this project. You're too numerous to list. Thank you all for your mentoring and support.

About the Author

Mo Villagran is an experienced business analytics veteran. She is well-versed in data analytics and the healthcare business across sectors, such as fraud detection, insurance pricing, and genetic research.

Mo leads initiatives on reporting efficiency, analysis pipelines, and cloud data architecture. In her current role, Mo established her company's first business analytics program and now manages cross-functional teams to deliver ETL processes and analytic frameworks that provide actionable insights for stakeholders and clients. She aims to deliver a world-class stakeholder experience in data analytics.

When she's not busy with data, she works on her sci-fi series that explores modern-day history and morality in a distant galaxy – The unmatched aspiration, the desperate attempt to maintain peace at all costs, the despair of reality, the regaining of the lost self, the broken system breaking again, etc.

Mo Villagran
https://movillagran.com

Data Concierge blog:
https://dataconcierge.co

DATA INSIGHTS DELIVERED

Thank You for Reading My Book!

Please take two minutes to leave a book review on Amazon by scanning the QR code below.

Thanks so much!
- Mo Villagran

Made in the USA
Las Vegas, NV
23 January 2024

84767997R00105